ESSAYS FOR THE THIRD CENTURY

Vincent Davis, Editor

THE CONTEXT OF
ENVIRONMENTAL POLITICS

Unfinished Business for America's Third Century

HAROLD SPROUT
MARGARET SPROUT

THE UNIVERSITY PRESS OF KENTUCKY

This book was written under the auspices of the
Center of International Studies, Princeton University. Other
books sponsored by the Center are listed following the Index at
the back of this book. The present book is one of several
products of a research and writing program supported jointly
by the Rockefeller Foundation and Princeton University.

ISBN: 0-8131-1374-1

Library of Congress Catalog Card Number: 77-84066

A statewide cooperative scholarly publishing agency
serving Berea College, Centre College of Kentucky,
Eastern Kentucky University, The Filson Club,
Georgetown College, Kentucky Historical Society,
Kentucky State University, Morehead State University,
Murray State University, Northern Kentucky University,
Transylvania University, University of Kentucky,
University of Louisville, and Western Kentucky University.

Editorial and Sales Offices: Lexington, Kentucky 40506

This book is dedicated to
our grandchildren

ROBERT, STEWART, & ANDREW

Our Personal Stake in the Future

Other books by Harold & Margaret Sprout

Toward a Politics of the Planet Earth (1971)
The Ecological Perspective on Human Affairs (1965)
Foundations of International Politics (1962)
Foundations of National Power (1945 & 1951)
Toward a New Order of Seapower (1940)
The Rise of American Naval Power (1939 & 1967)

Contents

Prologue
What This Book Is About

"Though it is easier, and perhaps far better not to begin at all, yet if a beginning is made it is here that most care is needed. Everything is inherent in the genesis."[1]

These words were written early in this century in a totally different context. However, they offer sensible advice to all authors. They admonish us to tell the readers we hope to reach what the book is about, and to disclose explicitly our perspective toward the issues with which it deals.

The book is focused on one of the numerous subcultures, or variants, of the mixture of beliefs, wants, expectations, laws, customs, practices, and other behaviors that in the aggregate compose what is rather loosely called the national culture. The book deals primarily with phenomena included in what we call the public-interest subculture. Specifically, it deals with some of the conditions that circumscribe the exercise of American public authority with regard to the physical habitat of the United States, of larger regions, and of the earth as a whole.

More precisely, our objective is to present a reasonably coherent word-picture of conditions and forces that now limit and seem likely to continue to affect American political responses to vulnerabilities—damage, risks, hazards—associated with a progressively deteriorating physical habitat. In short, as stated in the title, our theme is the context of environmental politics.

The policy problems subsumed in this context relate to many kinds of activities and relationships. These include some of the consequences of disruptive exploitations of nonhuman nature. They also include confrontations and interactions among individuals and organizations within the political community. In particular, we shall be concerned with factors that set the terms of permissible activities vis-à-vis the physical habitat.

These transactions reflect differences in conceptions of the public interest. They also reveal profound differences within the American community, and between that community and others, regarding past and continuing exploitation of the earth and regarding vistas of desirable and possible futures within the limits of our finite habitat.

We shall try to present these variant viewpoints fairly, but we make no claim of neutrality toward the progressive degradation of our magnificent country. We have been not only observers but also minor participants for three-quarters of a century in a milieu that seems to us to have changed and to be changing in ways both good and bad. We anticipate that still greater changes are likely to occur throughout and beyond America's third century. Some of these we would doubtless welcome. But we also envision changes that, unless arrested in time, could render our America a much less congenial habitat.

From what we have said thus far, it is evident that this book deals with the relations of *politics* and *environment*. These are slippery terms. Some dictionaries offer six or more definitions of politics. We have encountered nearly as many different definitions of environment. Each term is used in so many different contexts and with such diverse referents and connotations that it is essential to state as explicitly as possible, here at the outset, how *we* are using these terms.

We use *politics* in the broad sense to denote confrontations and interactions involved in exercise of authority, influence, and power on individuals, on the community as a whole, and in the inchoate world community of legally sovereign states. By *public authority* we mean legal competence to act concerning a given subject matter as the legitimate agent and spokesman of an organized community; in the United States, this includes several levels of jurisdiction: federal, regional, state, and local. Persons invested with such legal competence are by definition *public authorities*. We shall use this term in preference to government when we desire to emphasize that the reference is to the actions of biological persons rather than to the abstract concepts of government and state.

Even more confusing ambiguities enshroud the noun *environment* and the adjective *environmental*. All definitions have a common core: some organism or population is surrounded, or encompassed, by some combination of conditions judged to be significant for that organism or population. So far, clear enough; but usage in different contexts and vocabularies is inconsistent as well as ambiguous. Does environment (without a qualifying adjective) include only nonhuman objects and events? Does it include human organisms? Human institutions and relationships? Mental images derived from cognition of phenomena by those concerned, regardless of whether such images fit the situation in question?

We read that *the* environment is deteriorating, and that there is an *environmental* crisis. Some activists demand that *environmental* programs be postponed until more urgent "human" objectives are achieved. Others warn that environmental deterioration is approaching a "point of no return." *What* does this environmental crisis consist of? *What* is deteriorating? *What* should be postponed? *What* may be approaching some point of no return? Merely to ask these questions exposes the semantic ambiguities that enshroud environmental discussion.

Verbal usage varies among the natural sciences, social sciences, and moral philosophy, as it does in journalese, everyday speech, and still other vocabularies. In writing this book we have had to draw on all these sources, and others in addition. We have had to choose from conflicting definitions—or to redefine *environment* to suit the needs of this politically focused discussion. Our choice is to stick rather closely to the nontechnical usage of everyday speech which also approximates usage in the natural sciences. Though usage in no context is entirely consistent, natural scientists, journalists, and people generally tend to exclude strictly human phenomena from the idea of environment, especially human relationships such as status, discrimination, opportunity, and the like. Yet they rather generally include many conditions to which human activities contribute, such as depletions of natural resources; pollutions of air, water, and land; and other man-made changes in nonhuman nature. We shall often insert a qualifying adjective when the literary context seems unclear.

To return from this detour into semantics, humans have always had to cope with destructive phenomena of nature: floods, droughts, tornadoes, hurricanes, volcanic eruptions, earthquakes, epidemic diseases, and other such events. In our era, however, harmful impacts from the physical habitat are increasingly derivatives of human activities.

Economic practices and styles of personal living deplete the capital provided by nonhuman nature—fertile soil, fossil fuels, metals, and other earth materials; also they destroy beneficent plants, animals, microbes, and much else. Without these resources humans could not even exist. Depletions of this natural endowment produce residues and other conditions that contaminate air, water, and land, as also do many of the ways people live, work, and play.

Depletions and pollutions in countless combinations disrupt interrelations among humans, and between them and nonhuman nature. Consequences may be trivial or seriously harmful. Many of these latter are doubling in successively shorter periods. Whether particular changes are generating obstacles to continuing technological-economic growth, or even to long-term survival of industrial society, is endlessly debated. Disagreements also focus on whether scientific research and applied science can circumvent the "limits of the earth," and thereby enable humankind to eat their terrestrial cake and have it too.[2]

From this point debates fan out in numerous directions, leading to arguments regarding, among other topics, the essentials of a decently livable habitat; costs of maintaining such a habitat; impacts of these costs on other wants and commitments; impacts on the distribution of income and wealth within and among countries; environmental responsibilities of public authorities, and of business managements and other organizations and individuals; criteria for deciding what and how much environmental deterioration is tolerable; criteria for determining priorities among environmental and other claims on disposable resources; how to deal with disruptive exploitations of humankind's "estate in common," the oceans in particular; how to make any headway at all with global problems upon our politically fragmented earth in which the more than 145 legally sovereign polities differ profoundly in stage of technical and economic development, in natural-resource endowment, in ratio of people to accessible food and other essentials, in per capita income and wealth, and in images of what is desirable and possible.

Even this sketchy summary indicates how extensively public authorities are involved: in setting standards of environmental quality, achieving compliance to standards, allocating resources to achieve envisioned objectives, mobilizing public support for higher standards, and dealing with multinational and international conditions that contribute increasingly to accelerative deterioration of our terrestrial habitat.

In retrospect, it is noteworthy how long public authorities neglected these issues. It is likewise noteworthy that it took even longer for the "politics of environmental concern" to gain a secure foothold in education and research.[3] As recently as the early 1970s, most political scientists were leaving environmental problems pretty much alone.[4]

The political aspects of environmental protection are no more a monopoly of political scientists than ecology is a monopoly of environmental scientists, or than economic models are a monopoly of economists. Expert ecological diagnosis and prognosis are essential; likewise, creative science and engineering, and economic assessments and prescriptions. All of these, and still other specialties, are components of the milieu of environmental politics; but their outputs are beginnings, not ends. They are preliminaries to authoritative decisions regarding what and how much will actually be undertaken. Arresting environmental deterioration and protecting individuals and populations against damage and hazards therefrom require exercise of public authority. Such decisions include resolution of conflicting interests and choice among ethical as well as pragmatic considerations. Implicit upon every page of this book is our conviction that it is as relevant to the human future to prevent disruption of our physical and social environments as it is to avoid thermonuclear war, and that the organization and exercise of public authority is as germane in the former case as in the latter.

At one time we contemplated undertaking a global panorama of environmental politics, with descriptions of institutions and processes as well as of other influencing conditions and forces involved in different national settings and in the inchoate world community. However, the book that has finally taken shape is somewhat different in scope and focus.

Its scope is narrower in that it is focused primarily on problems confronting Americans in the third century of their republic. It is also narrower in the sense that one will find between these covers relatively little description of the myriad ways in which Americans (along with the rest of humankind) have been denuding, polluting, and disrupting their terrestrial habitat at accelerating rates. Since the 1960s, millions of words have been published describing these destructive activities. It seems unlikely that we could add much to this picture. Finally, our focus is narrower in that we give relatively little space to the institutions and processes of policymaking and administration. The omission does not reflect any doubt as to their importance. Again, this decision reflects a deliberate choice, influenced by the following considerations.

First, there is a lengthening list of books and shorter writings that are contributing new knowledge about the institutions and procedures of enacting and enforcing environmental legislation. Second, we have become increasingly impressed by the multiplicity of factors that affect environmental policies, in addition to those deriving from the physical environment itself, and in addition also to institutions and techniques of policymaking and administration. Speaking metaphorically, we feel a need to examine the context of environmental politics through a wider-angle lens. In this respect, the book is more broadly focused than the undertaking originally contemplated.

This wider-angle perspective includes the transnational context of environmental damage and risks: that is, those that derive from conditions and events outside the geographical space, jurisdiction, and effective influence and power of the United States. But here again, we have chosen not to include proposals and projects for changing the international order, changes that may be necessary for dealing effectively with problems that transcend the unilateral capabilities of all states. We have made this further limiting choice partly from considerations of space, but also because of recent expansion of research into the institutional requisites of a viable world order.[5]

It may or may not be demonstrable that "everything is connected to everything else," as Barry Commoner contends.[6] But the continuing deterioration of the life-supportive biosphere as well as the institutions and processes of making and administering policies, affects and is affected by many diverse conditions and forces that may seem at first to have little if any topical relevance.

We proceed from this broader perspective. We do so, among other reasons, because all the vulnerabilities that beset political communities impose claims on disposable resources, challenge existing allocations and priorities, and in still other ways disturb the status quo. These multiple claims have a bearing on what and how much is undertaken toward maintaining a decently livable habitat.

Our previous use of the expression *decently livable physical habitat* has evoked demands for a precise definition. Like such expressions as "acceptable environmental quality," *decently livable habitat* is difficult if not impossible to define very precisely, because its referent is a mixture of objective and subjective conditions. For example, what might seem decently livable to a destitute family might seem intolerable squalor to one accustomed to the amenities that affluence can buy.

In our usage, a decently livable habitat includes a core of elemental needs, such as adequate food, reasonably safe and healthful places to reside and work, personal safety in public places, and assurance of support in old age. In addition, we personally conceive a decently livable habitat to include conditions conducive to dignity and respect, minimal discrimination, and freedom to enjoy intangible values that do not encroach seriously on the values of others. However, without physical conditions conducive to safety and health, intangible values are unlikely to be attainable.

In exploring this and other ingredients of the context of environmental politics, we shall suggest numerous hypotheses intended to serve two related purposes: to enlarge understanding of our current and prospective predicaments, and to stimulate further investigation into some of the darker sectors of the environmental landscape.

Among other hypotheses, we shall argue, still somewhat tentatively, that *the multiple vulnerabilities and other conditions that affect responses to a progressively deteriorating physical habitat are symptoms of a malaise that has everywhere accompanied progression toward higher levels of technological and economic development*.

This and other propositions, some of which are previewed in chapter 1, affirm our conviction that environmental politics is *not* a congeries of more or less unrelated options and actions, but rather an interrelated component of a broader politics of multiple vulnerabilities that, in turn, is filling an expanding sector of the total politics of individual societies and of the inchoate world community.

If denudation and disruption of the physical habitat continue at current or higher rates, with progressively more damaging impacts on individuals and nations, environmental protection could escalate to an urgency comparable to what happened after Pearl Harbor. For the present, however, environmental protection remains one of many concerns; and demands for greater efforts and outlays compete, often at a disadvantage, with military, economic, humanitarian, and other demands that press on public authorities from diverse sources.

Before concluding our Prologue, we should emphasize that this is a controversial book about a very controversial subject. It deals with conditions and trends that seem likely to be still debatable after presently living people are long gone. We and our contemporaries are merely temporary observers of, and participants in, interrelated processes that, unless arrested or at least greatly decelerated during America's third century, could culminate in the "big bang" of terminal war, or in several kinds of more insidious but comparably destructive catastrophes.

There is continuing disputation about these hazards. Professional ecologists and other scientists, amateur naturalists, entrepreneurs, public authorities, and many from still other backgrounds and perspectives disagree profoundly as to what risks should be taken and what gambles should be prohibited.

Use of the word *should* here has special significance. The politics of environmental concern, like the politics of other concerns, includes a large ethical ingredient as well as empirical context and content. Philosophical postures—notions of right and wrong, good and bad, beneficial and harmful, tolerable and intolerable—are critical variables in determining what *should* be undertaken as well as what *can* presumably be accomplished *if* undertaken. For this reason alone, we find it difficult to exaggerate the salience of ethical-moral postures in any discussion of the context of environmental protection. In our view, such values loom so significantly in any calculation of consequences that we devote chapter 3 entirely to conflicting postures that go to the core of environmental policymaking.

What is known about the fragilities of the earth's life-supportive systems is considerable, but still only a fraction of what remains to be learned. Limited knowledge as well as myopic greed have contributed much to the progressive deterioration of our physical habitat. We assume that no sane person wants to destroy the earth's habitability. On the other hand, we find much evidence to suggest that pursuit of short-term gains often outweighs elemental prudence. A greater exercise of prudent caution in putting into circulation the results of innovative science and technology would have reduced the damage that link by link has forged the environmental crisis in which Americans, along with the rest of humankind, are now so deeply entangled.

⌒⊀1⊁⌒

"Our Plundered Planet"

THE EARTH is the human habitat. It provides, or transmits from the sun, the wherewithal that has enabled homo sapiens to rise from a precarious marginal subsistence to ever higher levels of knowledge, productivity, and other achievements. The sustaining conditions have included: an atmosphere containing enough but not too much free oxygen; thermal variations within the narrow limits of human physiological tolerance; adequate sunshine and rainfall; concentrated deposits of fossil fuels, earth-derived metals, and other materials of many kinds; and innumerable nonhuman species that contribute to human well-being and survival. If many of these beneficial elements were not being depleted, degraded, or destroyed at accelerating rates, most of the vulnerabilities with which this book is concerned might never have arisen.[1]

This deteriorative process has been going on for tens of thousands of years, but only within the past century or so has it acquired sufficient worldwide momentum to evoke much concern. Today, concern derives from (1) phenomena originating in outer space, (2) phenomena of terrestrial nature, and (3) human activities which contribute to environmental changes that react harmfully on individuals and populations.

Extraterrestrial phenomena have produced in the past, and continue to produce, harmful as well as beneficial impacts upon the earth and its inhabitants. Whether such phenomena have ever threatened to exterminate terrestrial life is indeterminable, and in any case outside the scope of this discussion.

Certain possibilities, which *are* relevant in this context, include terrestrial impacts of solar events. According to one hypothesis, variations in solar energy received upon the earth contribute to recurrent disruptive changes in climate. There are conjectures, and some evidence, that human activities may be raising the risk from this source. Such is the core of the disputed case against discharging fluorocarbons and other ozone-destroying chemicals into the atmosphere.[2]

When one turns to destructive phenomena of terrestrial nature, the picture is somewhat clearer. Such events provide emphatic reminders of human vulnerability to the yet uncontrollable forces of nature.[3] To provide some protection against these, men have built coastal breakwaters, riverside dikes, flood-control dams and reservoirs, earthquake-resistant buildings and bridges, and other protective structures. In some localities, public authorities have tardily prohibited further building upon dangerous sites, such as floodplains and unstable beaches. Some progress has been made toward predicting earthquakes, tropical storms, and other destructive natural events. Nevertheless, they still levy a heavy toll in lives and property.

American public authorities have repeatedly demonstrated superior ability to mobilize resources *after* disaster has struck; but responses to predicted hazards have been less impressive. There has been, and continues to be, notable reluctance to act preventively, especially when preventive action would reduce or threaten business profits, or entail substantial inconvenience for influential persons and groups.

Increasingly, dysfunctional changes in the biosphere (a technical term from biology that denotes those parts of the earth— land, water, atmosphere—where life can, or does actually, exist) are products or by-products of human activities. Wasteful consumption of energy and of high-grade raw materials is an example. So too is the discharge of toxic particles and gases from industrial plants, municipal incinerators, and automotive vehicles and planes. The same is true of ruinous denudation in the wake of timber cutting and surface mining, accumulations of solid wastes, and pollutions of the oceans, tidal waters, rivers, lakes, and underground aquifers by discharges of domestic and industrial wastes, as well as a lengthening list of other pollutants.

A recent study of topsoil loss in the United States provides explicit evidence of environmentally destructive use of land. That study concludes that "during the last 200 years, at least a third of the topsoil on the U.S. cropland has been lost." Some of this loss is attributed to nonagricultural activities, such as 2.5 million acres lost annually to highways, real estate developments, and the like. But the predominant cause is held to be erosion from overcropping, destructive field-layouts, and other practices that derive in considerable degree from growth of large-scale agribusiness conducted so as to take the largest possible short-term profit for absentee corporate shareholders.[4]

In many instances it is possible to identify a specific condition or event in nature, such as a tornado that destroys a swath of farmsteads, or an earthquake that wrecks a large city. In other instances, damage is attributable to strictly human sources, as when an industry discharges lethal chemicals into a public watercourse. More typically, damage and hazard result from some combination of natural events and human actions: for example, when a river overflows onto an adjoining built-up floodplain. Real estate developers have built upon hundreds, probably thousands, of these floodplains. Local, state, and federal agencies have usually been reluctant to prohibit such profitable intrusions. Then, when the flood comes, the damage is piously attributed to an "act of God" rather than to the negligence or timidity or ignorance of public authorities.

Attributing preventable damage to "an act of God" has long been a standard self-serving defense of ignorant or corrupt officials and entrepreneurs. Failure to take prudent preventive actions has long been sanctified by the traditional common law. The act-of-God plea has provided escape from legal liability. It is still accepted with remarkably little consideration of the irresponsible human contributions to the damage attributed to Divine Providence.

When one reads that drought and high winds (explained as "acts of God") cause destructive dust storms in the American semidry midcontinental plains, with serious damage to valuable land, a more realistic explanation would include the overcropping and other erosion-producing practices that destroy soil structures that previously helped to anchor the topsoil.

Often the situation is still more diffuse. In the example just cited, it may not be the farmers now being damaged whose practices contributed to the disaster, but farmers in previous years whose modes of tillage prepared the way for the destruction later attributed solely to drought and wind. Or, to cite a different but comparable exhibit of diffuse causation, we note that a single automobile user contributes only a tiny fraction of the pollutants that contaminate the air he breathes.

In sum, then, harmful changes in the habitat are likely to be the result of complex, often obscure, interactions that include natural phenomena and unanticipated or disregarded consequences of human activities spread over space and through time. A few or many may have contributed to those consequences; but the resultant damage may adversely affect the lives of perhaps uncounted millions who contributed little or nothing to the source of the damage that they have suffered and the continuing risk to which they and others are still exposed.

Historical Perspective

In prehistoric societies the physical habitat imposed formidable constraints on human achievement. In order to survive at all, it was generally necessary to adapt within a narrow range of choices. Ability to cope with nature expanded through time. There were setbacks, from natural disasters and from human ignorance and folly. There were eras of stagnation, even retrogression. Nevertheless, the trend was, and has continued to the present, in one direction: *from necessity to conform and accommodate to existing conditions in order to survive, toward enlarging ability to change environing conditions to suit human purposes.*

For tens of thousands of years this trend was generally slow and recurrently interrupted. With a few notable exceptions, knowledge of the earth, of its life-supportive processes and systems, and of outer space expanded very slowly. The same was true of such practical tasks as growing food and fiber, providing clothing and shelter, transporting goods and people, combating diseases, and much else.

However, even the knowledge and tools available in pre-industrial societies have been generally sufficient to leave a visible imprint upon the landscape, sometimes a destructive and lasting one. [5]

The destructive effects of human occupancy have been cumulative and sometimes accelerative. However, environmental depletions, pollutions, and disruptions have become critical in scale and in rate only within the past century or so, and these effects have become widely recognized and assessed only within the past few decades. With some local exceptions, human density was generally insufficient even in the recent past to destroy the recuperative forces of nature. [6]

Conversely, nearly everywhere, primitive technology contributed to back rending toil and a generally short life-span. It is easy today, in our largely mechanized society, to forget how recently primeval forests, stony landscapes, tough prairie sod, and other features of nature in North America and elsewhere were perceived as hostile elements by people dependent on human and animal muscles.

Even in technically and economically more advanced societies, severely limited power over large sectors of the physical habitat was a pervasive, grim reality within the memory of millions still living in the 1970s. In numerous respects, the milieu in 1900 resembled the world of the Roman Caesars more closely than it did the milieu to which most Americans are accustomed today.

By 1900, however, a radical transformation was well under way. A prime source of this transformation was the accelerating advance of scientific knowledge and its applications to engineering design and economic production. "It is hard to think of any advance in pure science which has not opened the door to a new advance in technology." [7]

Applied science accelerated the pace of economic innovation and productivity, first in Europe, then in North America and other parts of the world—a development that continues to this day. Rising economic production, in turn, increased the rate of extraction of fossil fuels and other nonrenewable resources that exist in nature. Expanding production concomitantly increased the quantity of noxious residues discharged into atmosphere and water and upon and into the land. These dysfunctional trends have been, and continue to be, further accelerated by concurrent decline of death rates and the resultant shortening periods in which population doubles and redoubles in the world as a whole.

Present knowledge indicates that the human species has existed for approximately a million years. The "median of several estimates" suggests a total population of about eight millions around 10,000 years ago. By A.D. 1, estimates suggest an increase to about 300 millions. [8] Estimates for the mid-seventeenth century indicate a further increase to something over 500 millions.

The Ehrlichs calculate that global population doubled on the average about every 1,500 years between 8000 B.C. and A.D. 1650. It took about 200 years to double the 1650 estimate; less than 100 years to double the population of 1850; and numerous projections for the year 2000 run higher than twice the total of 1950. The current doubling period is variously calculated to be between thirty and thirty-five years. [9] If even the lower estimates prove correct, world population would double nearly three times during the twenty-first century. That would yield a total of more than 40 billions by 2100.

Manifestly no such increase will actually occur. Population growth will be reduced in one way or another: by radical reduction of birthrates in the regions of rapid increase and/or by catastrophic increase of mortality from starvation, disease, or warfare.

At any given level of technological-economic development, increase of population manifestly puts a heavier burden upon the physical habitat. Hence, if both population and consumption are increasing simultaneously, these concurrent trends accelerate the rate as well as the magnitude of environmental denudation and disruption more than either trend by itself. That is substantially what is happening today. Not only are more societies acquiring more efficient tools wherewith to exploit the earth; nearly everywhere, there are increasing numbers to do the exploiting, and befoul air, water, and land in the process. [10]

That is, the higher the level of a society's exploitive capabilities, *plus* the greater and more diverse its economic output, *plus* the higher the ratio of people to accessible energy and materials, *the more severely have the activities of that society's members depleted and polluted their physical habitat, and (in some instances) contributed to environmental degradation beyond their own geographic space.* In chapter 6 we shall add another variable to this proposition: the large and apparently increasing rates of depletion and pollution attributable to diversion of resources to production of military hardware—an allocation that commands high priority even in poverty-ridden countries, most of whose inhabitants are living at a level of bare subsistence and recurrent famine.

The hazards of spreading industrialism and population growth in a finite habitat have not gone unnoticed. One early prophet was Thomas Malthus (1766–1834). Another was George Perkins Marsh (1801–1882), New England lawyer and businessman, diplomat and amateur earth scientist. In 1864 Marsh voiced concern lest advances in industrialization might so deplete the earth "as to threaten depravation [*sic*], barbarism, and perhaps even extinction of the human species." [11]

Passing over a number of other seers ahead of their time, we come to Fairfield Osborn who (in 1948) warned that what "man has done . . . to the face of the earth and the accumulated velocity with which he is . . . [continuing to do it] is destroying his own life sources." [12] In the same year, naturalist William Vogt likened the human predicament to a person wearing "shoes two sizes too small." [13] The predominant reaction to Osborn and Vogt, as to other prophets of environmental disaster, was to shrug off their warnings as simpleminded nonsense.

Still in the same year (1948), professional ecologist Aldo Leopold anticipated one of the controversial issues of today, saying: "A system of conservation based solely on economic self-interest is hopelessly lopsided. It tends to ignore, and thus to eliminate, many elements . . . that lack commercial value [such as clean air and water], but that are (as far as we know) essential. . . . It assumes, falsely, I think, that the economic parts of the biotic clock will function without the uneconomic parts." [14]

Leopold was congratulated by reviewers for his "beautiful writing," his "heart-warming" empathy with nature, and more of the same. But remarkably few paid attention to his assessment of the disasters latent in the ruthless plundering of the natural endowment.

Moving ahead to 1955, at a conference convened to assess "man's role in changing the face of the earth," a few speakers warned of the limits of the earth; and the geographer Carl Sauer introduced the novel idea that "what we need more perhaps is an ethic and esthetic under which man, practicing the qualities of prudence and moderation, may indeed pass on to posterity a good Earth." [15]

Three years later, biologist Paul Sears, while denying any hostility to the then-burgeoning space program, added the caveat that "our future security may depend less upon priority . . . [in exploring outer space] than upon our wisdom in managing the space in which we live." [16]

Indications of expanding concern began to surface in the later 1950s. This concern gained momentum in response to several shocking incidents in the following decade. If public apathy was the reward of Osborn, Vogt, Leopold, Sauer, Sears, and others who had sounded the alarm, the opposite was the impact of

Rachel Carson. Despite efforts of hostile interests, her book *Silent Spring* was published in 1963. Its main theme is well known. Long-persisting pesticides, DDT in particular, save food and fiber crops from predatory insects, and humans from malaria and certain other diseases. But these long-lived poisons also accumulate in food chains and eventually turn up on our own dinner tables.

Carson and her book were attacked by manufacturers of pesticides, by farmers' organizations, by numerous doctors of medicine, and by a mixed assortment of industrial and academic scientists. All this uproar, however, failed to suppress Carson's message. On the contrary, it helped mightily to spread it far and wide. A retrospective survey concludes that *Silent Spring* "made large areas of government and public aware for the first time of the interrelations of all living things and the dependence of each on a healthful environment."[17] This may be a slight exaggeration, for other events contributed simultaneously to the same end.

One of these was the widely publicized strontium 90 episode —the contamination of milk supplies by radioactive fallout from weapons testing, thousands of miles from the test site in western United States. This discovery culminated in 1963 (the same year as *Silent Spring*) in a treaty driving American and Russian nuclear-weapons testing underground.[18]

The oil spills from the wreck of the *Torrey Canyon* off the southern coast of England (1967) and from oil well accidents in the Santa Barbara Channel two years later added fuel (so to speak) to a brightening fire of media publicity. Front-page headlines and prime-time television alerted millions to environmental troubles: not only oil spills but also persistent air pollution overhanging large areas of industry and motor traffic; recurrent lethal smogs; severe contamination of lakes, rivers, and tidal waters; spreading heaps of junk and litter; and other evidences of a deteriorating habitat.

Americans reacted in various ways. A minority—always a small one—took pollutions seriously. From these concerned citizens came scores of books and hundreds of articles, organizations to inform the public and to press for protective legislation, suits in the courts to abate pollutions, ecologically oriented teaching in schools and colleges, local recycling projects, and other activities directed toward arresting the processes that were perceived to be insidiously making our habitat less habitable.

A few scientists and numerous amateur activists envisioned irreversible catastrophe unless drastic reforms should be undertaken soon to halt the assaults on the life-supportive processes of the biosphere. Others doubted that doomsday was imminent, but nevertheless anticipated worsening troubles from rapidly increasing world population, misdirected engineering, misguided economic growth, accelerative depletion of high-grade natural resources, and industrial practices and personal lifestyles that separately and in combination were eroding the American condition and prospect.

It was this many-faceted piecemeal degradation of the biosphere as much as the possibility of ultimate irreversible catastrophe that impelled environmental scientists and others to warn that humankind (Americans along with the rest) were already far advanced in a dangerous and worsening crisis.

We know of no evidence that any majority took seriously the diagnosis of environmental crisis. Many admitted the existence of polluted air and water and other environmental disorders, but insisted that there was nothing to justify drastic restrictions that might reduce business profits, produce unemployment, or otherwise react adversely on personal wants and expectations. Most, it would seem, simply shrugged off the whole business as a passing fad. Predominant attitudes, in short, ignored or belittled present damage and predictions of future disasters.

Numerous spokesmen for the poor and destitute also challenged the diagnosis of critical urgency. They attacked demands for environmental protection as a red herring invented by affluent elites to divert attention from their chronic failure to deal effectively with more urgent "human" problems. A few advocates of environmental protection warned that this goal could not be politically isolated from other urgent tasks, especially humanitarian tasks, that continue to confront American society, an issue to which we shall return in chapter 8.

Many Problems: One Crisis

There has been a conspicuous propensity in America and elsewhere to treat depletions, pollutions, and ecological disruptions as more or less unrelated phenomena. This compartmented thinking may be attributable in some degree to the chronological order in which these respective phenomena were brought to public attention.

In the late 1960s we began collecting environmental news and commentaries. Within a few months we were swamped with paper devoted almost entirely to pollutions. Then abruptly in the 1970s attention shifted to depletions, especially to shortages of motor fuel, heating oil, and natural gas, and to the fantastic inflation of prices for these and other essentials of our industrial-urban-suburban society. As shortages and inflation captured attention, it became apparent that most reporters, editors, politicians, businessmen, and citizens generally, saw few if any significant connections between depletions and pollutions. Even numerous environmental activists failed to recognize (or at least to emphasize) these connections.

This failure was exemplified by one of the typical responses to the energy shortage of 1973–1974. Numerous gross polluters, harassed by tightening restrictions, and prospects of still stiffer antipollution standards, voiced the hope that queues at gasoline pumps, colder offices and homes, skyrocketing utility bills, and higher prices for nearly everything else, would break the back of the fanatical "environmental crusade"—exhibiting apparent failure to perceive any significant relationship between energy and pollutions.

Even today we find remarkably few Americans who yet seem to grasp this connection and its significance—always excepting professional ecologists and a scattering from other backgrounds. For example, how many of your acquaintances comprehend that a great deal of energy is expended in producing more usable energy in order to produce more raw materials from which to manufacture more automobiles that pollute the air; and that still more energy is consumed in the process of reducing automotive pollutions to tolerable levels? How many understand that most of the processes of generating electric power, and all of the processes of smelting ores, combining metals into alloys, making glass, growing food, indeed producing nearly everything we use, not only consume energy but also leave residues that must be disposed of somewhere, and that additional expensive energy is required to recycle residues or otherwise dispose of them in ways that do not further worsen pollutions of air or water or land?

One could add more examples from virtually every sector of industrial society. The ones already cited should suffice to demonstrate that environmental depletions and pollutions are not phenomena packageable, so to speak, in separate containers. Their interrelatedness is more comparable to that of the parts of an engine or of the interacting divisions of a large corporation. To summarize some of the relational patterns that are often missed in newspaper reports, editorials, popular books and articles, and in the formulation and enactment of business and governmental policies:

$$\text{depletions} \rightarrow \text{pollutions}$$

That is, extraction and processing of energy and materials produce residues that pollute air, water, and land. Also,

$$\text{eliminating and reducing pollutions} \rightarrow \text{depletions}$$

That is, it takes energy and materials to eliminate or contain within tolerable limits the pollutions resulting from exploitation of energy and materials. Finally,

$$\begin{matrix} \text{depletions} \\ \uparrow \downarrow \quad \rightarrow \text{systemic disruptions} \\ \text{pollutions} \end{matrix}$$

Interactions between depletions and pollutions produce changes in the biosphere (for example, damage to or destruction of habitats of plant and animal species) that often adversely affect the human population.

We conclude this opening chapter with a preview of a few of the propositions that identify specifically the multiplicity of interrelated conditions and forces that affect what is undertaken and accomplished toward arresting progressive spoliation of the physical habitat.[19]

This preview is intended to serve two purposes. It introduces major themes of subsequent chapters. But perhaps more important, it should help to enlarge the framework of inquiry and analysis, and thereby contribute to better understanding of the tasks involved in maintaining a decently livable physical habitat.

These previewed propositions include some that are still conjectural. However, despite the elementary quality of a few and the conjectural indeterminacy of others, all are links in chains of observation, study, and cogitation that have taken us into some of the less investigated areas of the landscape of environmental politics.

1. It is axiomatic that technological-economic development (which throughout this preview we designate simply as TE-D) entails functional specialization; and specialization usually increases the variety and quantity per capita of goods and services produced—an effect called economic growth in current idiom.

2. The rate of TE-D varies not only with the application of new knowledge but also with the accessibility and price of energy, materials, equipment, and labor, especially energy in concentrated forms derived to date chiefly from coal, petroleum, natural gas, nuclear fission (perhaps increasingly), and a few other sources.

3. With very few exceptions if any, the higher the society's technical capabilities, and the more productive its economy, and the more dense its population and higher the rate of increase, the more rapidly and extensively have its members depleted the energy and materials derived from land, water, and atmosphere to which they have access.

4. With no exceptions, TE-D has entailed increasing accumu-

lations of residues, many of which cause damage to human and nonhuman populations, and continuing hazards of future damage. Since about 1950, the rates of depletion and pollution have risen sharply.

5. Accelerative exploitation of nature has been rationalized by a philosophical posture that posits humankind in the role of predestined conquerors and masters of the earth and its subhuman populations and rejects the notion of limits to profitable exploitation within any time-frame of concern to currently living people.

6. TE-D multiplies interrelatedness: that is, the more specialized a local or larger community becomes, the greater become the interdependencies among its members, and usually also their collective dependence on energy, materials, fabricated goods, and services supplied from a distance—increasingly from places beyond their geographic space and legal jurisdiction.

7. Innovations that generate serious hazards, especially long-term open-ended hazards, such as those inherent in nuclear-fission power and genetic research and engineering, are rational only on the assumption of foolproof security virtually forever against technical malfunction, illicit interventions, and human failures.

8. Such stability has never been even remotely approached and is inconceivable without a degree of regimentation, including destruction of personal freedom that would be totally incompatible with the premises upon which the American republic was founded and which most of its citizens continue to value highly.

9. TE-D, beyond some point that varies from country to country, entails rising costs per capita in order to keep the community functional, including the price of maintaining a sufficiently supportive physical habitat.

10. Rising costs of reducing or containing vulnerabilities from deteriorating changes in the physical habitat compete with a multiplicity of claims on public funds from other sources; thus the budgetary process is the site of priority decisions that deter-

mine what and how much shall be allotted to environmental repair and protection.

11. Though we are concerned in this book primarily with the context of American environmental politics, we are inclined to believe that the environmental implications of TE-D are universal.

12. Furthermore, not even preindustrial societies can escape disturbing impacts of industrialism beyond their borders. Trends in weapons and traffic in arms; unprecedented mobility of goods, people, and messages; competition for energy and materials; organization of production and commerce; ambition to emulate the industrial giants; population increase yet to be significantly curtailed—all these and still other conditions and forces contribute to lock even the least industrially developed societies into a global interdependence.

13. No national polity can unilaterally protect its citizens from all harmful impacts of environmentally disruptive practices in other countries. None can unilaterally prevent excessive foreign exploitation and degradation of the global ocean. For these and other reasons the global biosphere has become in important economic and ecological respects a single system. This is so de spite continued political fragmentation of the earth, and the tribalistic attitudes and behaviors of all national populations. From these conditions it follows that maintenance of even a minimally livable physical habitat will require concerted international action on a scale beyond anything seriously contemplated as yet.

Implicit throughout this synoptic preview has been the premise that shrinkage of the role of government is improbable. Our expectation is rather a continuing expansion of that role, both domestically and internationally. It will require a great deal more than persuasion to modify the widely prevailing exploitive attitudes and norms that sustain the wasteful and environmentally disruptive practices of industry and the styles of living that permeate American culture. Only government can mobilize and reallocate resources on a scale necessary to arrest the insidious drift toward ruination of the earth. Barring radical changes in the international legal-political order, primary responsibility for protection against environmentally linked damage and hazards originating abroad will continue to rest upon national governments. Finally, with possible minor exceptions, only organized public authority can command the *power* necessary to insure compliance with standards of environmental quality if less coercive incentives prove insufficiently effective.

～2 ～

Questions for Policymakers

THE PROLOGUE and chapter 1 have offered a quick tour of our deteriorating physical habitat. We have identified some of the conditions that do, or should, inspire programs of repair and protection. Suppose, now, that you are a member of Congress, a state legislature, or a local council, or that you are some other official charged with responsibility for maintaining a decently livable environment. What questions would you need to consider in order to act wisely in the public interest? Assuming you are a methodical person, how would you envision the sequential stages in rational policymaking? How would you decide what should, or can, be undertaken to protect yourself, your constituents, and your posterity from serious harm arising from denudations, pollutions, or other dysfunctional changes in your locality and in the larger world with which your community interacts?

These are the kinds of questions to which this chapter is addressed. It would be pretentious to call it a guide. But we shall try to identify logical sequential stages in the process of reaching policy decisions, and to formulate some of the questions that should be taken into account at each stage.

Since environmental politics, like all politics, is concerned primarily with problems reaching into the future, environmental policymaking, again like all policymaking, involves uncertainties inherent in all futuristic undertakings. How to deal with this element of indeterminacy is also considered in our discussion of questions for policymakers.

The stages of environmental policymaking can be conceived and classified in various ways. The typology suggested here reflects the sequential order of rational procedure as we conceive this to be. Questions are grouped under the following categories: (1) assessment of damage incurred; (2) calculation of hazards implicit in the situation; (3) technical remedies available or in prospect; (4) procedural options; (5) criteria of decisions; (6) feedback and reassessment of results.

The first and second categories are respectively diagnostic and prognostic. They direct attention to such questions as: (a) What kind of damage or hazard is at issue? Bodily damage to the person? Damage to reputation? To property? Or what? (b) How many people are affected, or likely to be? One? A few? Hundreds? Thousands? Millions? The human population in toto? (c) How much time do we have before action is necessary? Is it imperative to do something immediately? Or is there time for further investigation? If so, how much? (d) How large an area is involved, or likely to be? A village? Larger town or region? Entire country? Several countries? The earth as a whole? (e) How severe is the damage incurred or anticipated? Trivial? Substantial? Catastrophic? (f) What is the state of the problem? Damage contained? Spreading? Out of control? Uncontrollable? (g) To what specific source(s) is the damage or hazard attributed? What hypothesis, or conflicting hypotheses, purport to explain how assessed damage occurred, or how predicted damage is likely to occur? (h) How much information is available? How reliable is it? What essential data are missing?

Damage incurred (category 1) merges into continuing or predicted risk of future damage (category 2). Calculation of risk involves, as indicated above, most of the questions involved in assessment of damage incurred, but with a salient difference. Risks are calculable, not from more or less hard data, but from assumptions regarding future conditions. Hence, calculation of risks always entails uncertainties that are generally greater than those encountered in diagnosis of damage already incurred.

Furthermore, as should be expected, uncertainty increases as calculations are pushed toward more distant futures. The issue of uncertainty receives further attention in the chapter's concluding section.

Compensation after damage incurred is often inadequate, and sometimes meaningless. A worker who dies or is permanently disabled from lung disease contracted by prolonged exposure to toxic chemicals in his working place is manifestly beyond help. Recognition of this limitation is gradually shifting the emphasis from redress to prevention, with consequent increase of uncertainty and room for disagreement. Nevertheless, advances in applied science—new industrial reagents, new synthetic fabrics and other materials, new food additives, and much else—are expediting this shift. Every step in this direction puts a higher premium on reliable calculation of hazards. Such calculations are complicated, and the futuristic assumptions built into them lead to different conclusions regarding harmful side effects. Despite uncertainties and disputations, however, calculations of risks are increasingly important ingredients of the context of policymaking.

Diagnosis and prognosis of the condition to be corrected is logically the first step. Most people turn to a medical doctor when stricken with illness. It seems comparably sensible to rely on the relevant specialists for diagnosis and prognosis of environmental damage and hazards. Limitations of knowledge and data impose uncertainty, and comparably qualified specialists may disagree. Nevertheless, judgments of relevant specialists are, at least prima facie, more trustworthy, within the boundaries of their specialty, than opinions informed by a less relevant specialty, or by snippets of news or the glossy propaganda of self-serving parties.

But expert judgments are not substitutes for operational decisions. Such judgments do not guarantee effective action, or any action at all. This is especially so if effective action entails spending large sums for which other urgent claims compete, or if it threatens amenities that the affluent have come to consider necessities and the poor and destitute yearn to acquire.

In category 3, technical remedies available or in prospect are essential bridges between diagnosis/prognosis and authoritative decisions. It seems reasonable to anticipate that innovative technology will be as essential to maintaining a decently livable habitat as it has been contributory to denudation, pollution, and disruption of that habitat to date. From this perspective, rational choice of remedial and preventive strategies involves considering such questions as: (a) What alternative technologies—knowledge, skills, equipment, processes—are relevant to the task under consideration? (b) Are these technologies available, or in course of development? (c) What harmful consequences may their application entail? (d) What damage and hazards are beyond reach of currently or prospectively available technical solutions?

These questions, to which others could be added, are among the ingredients of the impact assessments increasingly required before major construction on large projects is undertaken. The same questions are involved in evaluating alternative techniques for repairing or arresting environmental deterioration already occurring. In both types of cases such assessments pose uncertainties similar to those involved in calculating risks in general.

Some in our midst query whether environmental engineering has done, or can do, more good than harm. A few reject "technological fixes" altogether, though such is plainly an eccentric view. Most Americans exhibit a faith in engineering that approaches a gospel of salvation by innovative technology.

Many, like ourselves, find neither extreme credible. On the one hand, it will require much besides innovative engineering to extricate us from the continuing insidious slide toward environmental ruin. On the other hand, we plainly cannot manage at all without superior scientists and engineers. Most environmental problems today present technical questions and complexities. Some require highly sophisticated knowledge and techniques. Our dependence on the advance of engineering is evident in the need to burn fossil fuels more economically, to develop reasonably safe alternative sources of energy, to recycle more used materials, to invent substitutes for depleted natural materials, and to cope with many other facets of the progressive denudation of the earth.

The same dependence is evident in our need to deal with pollutions: whether the task is to clean up automotive exhausts, to reduce the roar of jet planes, to produce less dangerous pesticides, to develop less hazardous methods of handling industrial reagents and residues, or to prevent a long and lengthening list of other environmental pollutions. Scientific research and innovative engineering are, and will continue to be, essential elements of the context of environmental politics.

Arguments regarding the contributions and proper role of pure and applied science involve questions relevant to all specialties. These, in turn, evoke the question: Who should be responsible for deciding what research and engineering projects shall be permitted? This question carries important ethical as well as purely pragmatic connotations. It does so especially when reasonably calculable side effects of contemplated research and development include large, possibly monstrous, hazards to which a particular population will be exposed, and which may even alter the survival-odds of the human species.

Such considerations give additional significance to questions implicit in category 4—procedural options. Clearly, the first of these questions—(a)—is the location of legal competence to decide what may be undertaken. Other questions include: (b) whether to do something or nothing—a question that involves calculating the consequences of inaction as well as those of proposed actions, (c) whether to opt for direct regulation backed by coercive sanctions, or for less coercive incentives; (d) at what jurisdictional level to proceed—an issue of special relevance when the source of danger is partially outside the legal jurisdiction of the authorities contemplating need for some kind of action; (e) whether existing institutions are adequate, and if judged not to be, what changes are feasible as well as needed.

Choices among procedural options evoke historic arguments about the proper role of government. On this issue, marketplace economics exhibits a bias in favor of strategies that minimize direct governmental regulation and maximize private initiatives, a bias about which more will be said in chapter 3. Here, it is sufficient to note that economic prescriptions, like ecological assessments and environmental engineering, are beginnings, not ends. They are preliminaries to authoritative decisions and administrative actions, with the police power of government in the background to enforce compliance if necessary. It is no disparagement of the importance of ecological diagnoses, pure and applied science, and economic prescriptions to emphasize that public authorities are charged with legal responsibility for determining what actions best serve the public interest.

Category 5, criteria of decisions, is addressed to the nature and scope of the constraints imposed by the political system and the social order to which politicians are responsible and responsive. Category 5 thus directs attention to such issues as: (a) relative costs of different modes of protection; (b) vulnerabilities from diverse *other* sources that compete for public attention, and for available funds; (c) amount of disposable funds for all public purposes; (d) priorities among competing claims for chronically insufficient disposable funds; (e) other claimants—individuals, organizations, civil and military agencies, and others—to whom politicians are likely to be responsive; (f) philosophical postures —attitudes, ethical principles, priorities, etc.—prevailing among those who rule and those to whom rulers are responsible.

Even if account is duly taken of what is politically expedient as well as technically possible and economically workable, the basic issue of decisional criteria remains unresolved. Those who formulate and strive for adoption of environmental programs, and public authorities who decide what is to be undertaken, confront a thicket of ethical questions, among which are: (a) Who *should* set quality standards for air, water, land, noise, etc.? (b) Who *should* decide whether grossly wasteful consumption shall be tolerated? (c) Who *should* determine who shall pay for a safer, more healthful, cleaner, and otherwise better habitat? (d) Who *should* decide how much responsibility the well-to-do shall bear for the poor and destitute in our own country and abroad? (e) *Should* "ability to pay" determine who gets food, who goes hungry, and who is allowed to starve? (f) *Should* presently living, relatively affluent elites opt for reprieve from personal inconvenience by passing a heavier burden to generations yet unborn? (g) Who *should* determine priorities between environmental sources of damage and hazard and other claims on disposable resources?

Such ethical questions lurk in every serious discussion of our deteriorating habitat and in every proposal for more environmental protection. These questions pose in various ways the generic question of who and what *should* be entitled to priority when the existing distribution of income and wealth, structure of taxation, and productivity of the economy generate insufficient resources to cover all urgent needs.

Neither ecological projections nor environmental engineering nor conventional benefit-cost formulas can provide answers to these ethical questions. If they are left to entrepreneurs—producers, merchants, real estate developers, bankers, and others—or to the personal choices of other individuals, experience suggests that these issues will generally be resolved in favor of personal short-term gains—chiefly in money and what money can buy. Only public authorities are formally and explicitly obligated to put the common interest ahead of private interests. They may do their job intelligently or stupidly, honestly or corruptly, but there is no one else to carry this responsibility, some marketplace economists to the contrary notwithstanding.

For this reason if for no other, it seems to us pure fantasy to anticipate any shrinkage of the role of public authority in protecting individuals, nations, and the inchoate world community against progressively destructive exploitation of the earth. The relevant generic question, we repeat, is not *whether* government will play an expanding role. It is rather *how* those invested with legal authority will perform. What values and priorities will guide their decisions and the manner of their administrative follow-through? This is the ultimate issue to which category 5 is addressed.

Category 6, feedback and reassessment, focuses on the need for periodic reexamination of results achieved from ongoing programs, and on the importance of continuous monitoring of environmental changes both domestic and international. Feedback from an ongoing operation may uncover inadequacies or even definitely injurious side effects. But feedback may or may not be heeded. Hence, the importance of emphasizing this continuously important ingredient of the context of environmental politics.

Subjectivity and the Consequences Thereof

If one defines harmful impacts of environing conditions in terms of personal sensations (psychological state, mental image, etc.), he is manifestly identifying phenomena different from actual affliction with disease, loss of property, or other damage diagnosable without reference to the perceptions of the individual(s) in question. In the first category, the reference is to the mental responses of the affected person(s); in the latter, to states of affairs that affect him (them) adversely, regardless of whether or how these are perceived and construed or comprehended by such person(s).[1]

How to infer mental images of another person has occupied philosophers and jurists for centuries. We do not propose to go further here than to state three points relevant to the present discussion: first, the images and reactions of individuals are often discrepant from actual situations to which they are reacting; second, images that do not fit actuality may be just as operative as those that do; and third, the consequences of discrepancy between the milieu as cognized and as it actually is (or may become) may be trivial but are often substantial and sometimes severely harmful to the person or population under consideration.

Subjective sensations of vulnerability are designated by many words in common use, such as annoyance, irritation, frustration, revulsion, sense of deprivation, anxiety, or fear. Mental images discrepant from actuality may originate in delusions and hallucinations of a disordered personality or in physical handicaps such as impaired hearing or vision. Or discrepancy may derive from external conditions to be considered further in a moment. The point here is simply that, whatever the source of discrepancy, it is the individual's cognition of reality that evokes his sensations of damage or other mental states.[2]

Sensations of damage incurred merge into anxieties and fears about the future: such as fear of natural phenomena (lightning, earthquakes, tornadoes, floods, and so on), fear of hunger and destitution, fear of bodily harm, fear of illness, fear of producing deformed offspring, anxiety for the safety and fitness of one's children, and, in recent years in the United States and a few other countries, a gradually surfacing sense of unease regarding degeneration of the physical habitat.

From the viewpoint of an external observer, conditions may or may not appear to justify a particular person's expressed fears and anxieties. For example, the low ratio of accidents to total miles of air travel may or may not seem to justify the sense of anxiety that a given person may exhibit when contemplating a journey by airliner. However, it is the latter's sense of insecurity, regardless of statistical probability, that constitutes reality for him.

Subjective discontents may be idiosyncratic and eccentric, or they may reflect attitudes that prevail widely within a community. According to conventional wisdom, attitudes and complaints that are widely shared stand a better chance of becoming live political issues. However, when one shifts from the question Whose discontents are likely to command effective attention? to the question What discontents *should* receive attention? a controversial issue emerges. Should personal taste receive any consideration at all in the realm of political action?

Taste and distaste are aesthetic concepts. They enter into many complaints about littered roadsides, urban and suburban sprawl, piped-in "music" in supermarkets, noisy neighbors, decaying garbage, and many other sources of discontent. It has also been argued that there is an aesthetic element—that is, an experience of beauty or other contentment—in relief or anticipation of relief from deprivation, felt loss, anxiety, and fear.[3]

For many people the Empire State Building, the Grand Coulee

Dam, the Golden Gate Bridge, a superhighway, a nuclear power plant, a blackboard covered with mathematical equations, and other artifacts of advanced learning and technology evoke a sense of beauty. For these people, such things may be more emotionally appealing than the Grand Canyon, Mount Rainier, wild geese in flight, or other phenomena of nature. A square meal may seem more beautiful than great art to a starving person, just as the latter may be more emotionally evocative to persons accustomed to three square meals every day.

Such variations in personal taste inject an element of indeterminacy into arguments about the "quality of life" and about the requisites of an "optimal" or even "acceptable" environment. This indeterminacy shows up in many situations. For example, we never cease to be surprised, even shocked, by the indifference of some of our friends to things that give us a sense of contentment—such as, say, a deep blue sky, the earthy smell of our garden in spring, conversing endlessly about this book before a fireplace fueled with our own hand-sawed wood, and so on. On the other hand, we suspect that many of our friends are baffled by our dislike of cities, noisy cocktail parties, and the unceasing rumble of jetliners overhead, as well as by our aversion to apartment-style living, and much else.

What we are leading up to is that some essentially aesthetic criteria are ingredients of everyone's responses to his milieu, and that these vary from person to person and from culture to culture. We are also suggesting that arguments and counterarguments regarding the state and prospects of the physical habitat, and of the quality of life attainable therein, are permeated with just such culture-conditioned and personally variant criteria.

To the contention that politicians and bureaucrats should leave aesthetic values to individuals and to the marketplace, our response is that to do so is to leave these criteria to real estate developers, automobile manufacturers, cattle farmers, lumber companies, advertising agencies, television programmers, and others whose top priority is likely to be maximization of short-term profits. We envision a middle ground in which the ethos of the marketplace makes room for aesthetic values not calculable by the arithmetic of short-term profit and loss. Norms of what is desirable and undesirable, what is good and bad taste, are embedded in the Anglo-American common law, especially in the concepts of public and private nuisances, and today in an expanding corpus of environmental legislation at all levels of government.

Aesthetic norms can and do change through time. But in any era, more or less generally prevailing standards of taste influence actions of public authorities as well as the behavior of private citizens. Provided elemental needs are reasonably assured, most people seem to desire something in addition. Is it, then, unreasonable to anticipate that intangible values, including those considered purely aesthetic, will continue to influence environmental legislation and administration?[4]

Personal discontents—that is, the subjective aspect of vulnerabilities—are only one side of the coin. The other side is the objective aspect. As previously noted, an individual or population may suffer damage without premonition thereof, or even without awareness that damage has occurred. Hazards may proliferate and portend serious damage whether or not such risks are anticipated by potential victims.

Discrepancies between perceptions of vulnerabilities—both damage and hazards—form parts of the setting of regulatory actions in all environments. For this reason it is worth considering some of the types of situation which turn on such discrepancies.

In some instances, neither the potential victim nor percipient external observers have recognized hazards, because *such hazards were indeterminable in the then existing state of knowledge.* Field workers, for example, have suffered disablement or premature death from contact with toxic pesticides before the severity of that hazard became reasonably well confirmed. For centuries people have become ill from dietary and sanitary practices that no one then knew to be harmful. One could cite examples indefinitely to illustrate this principle.

Hazards may be recognized but their severity discounted because *evidence is inconclusive and experts disagree*. One of many current examples is the continuing dispute regarding climatic changes attributable to increasing discharge of CO_2 into the atmosphere.

In another category, *evidence of risk is well established but inaccessible, or not easily accessible, to persons likely to be harmed*. Persons constantly board airliners unaware of the quality of maintenance upon which their lives depend. Very few people who eat commercially processed food have access to the factories and kitchens involved. This list too could be extended indefinitely.

Habituation is another source of discrepancy between image and actuality (or predicted actuality) of hazard. There is evidence that people will accept restrictions, even onerous ones, if they are sufficiently anxious or frightened. But there is also evidence that many who are subjected to gradually changing conditions—changes that insidiously undermine health, shorten life, or erode efficiency and other values—adjust, often with scarcely any awareness that they are doing any adjusting. They may even forget in time that conditions were ever any different.

Adjustment to worsening air pollution offers innumerable exhibits of the insidious character of this adaptive process. Some individuals experience difficulty breathing. Others suffer headaches, eye irritation, sinus congestion, or simply do not feel fit. But the characteristic response is still to dismiss such symptoms as of little or no consequence. Most individuals, including many presumably competent medical specialists, tend to "accept the [condition of the air, or other dysfunctional condition of the environmental] status quo as 'natural.'" [5]

Another source of discrepancy between cognition and actuality (or predicted actuality) is the *deliberate withholding or distorting of relevant information by one party to a transaction*. Such deception is the essence of camouflage. It is commonplace in commercial advertising. It is sanctified in the infamous common-law doctrine of "buyer beware."

Real estate transactions offer especially rich opportunities for such deception. Dealers have sold houses without revealing known weaknesses of construction. Developers have sited residential septic systems upon impervious subsoil or bedrock, and then sold the property without warning the purchaser of the hidden source of virtually certain future trouble. One could cite innumerable commercial transactions that exemplify this kind of subjective-objective discrepancy.

Sometimes *risks are communicated, even well publicized, but still disregarded*. Consider the following hypothetical, but not untypical, case. Potential buyer *B* considers purchasing a residence overlooking a river. Actually, the property is located upon the river's floodplain, periodically inundated. *B* knows nothing about floodplains, and the salesman avoids the subject. Hence, at this stage, *B* is the victim of deliberate deception. However, a third party, a hydrological engineer, enlightens *B*. The latter listens to the warning, but decides there really cannot be much risk from such a placid stream. His image of the prospect is thus discrepant from the expert's judgment. But it is *B*'s image, not the expert's judgment, that guides his decision to purchase the property. However, when the river overflows, as predicted, and ruins *B*'s house, it is the objective reality, not *B*'s defective image thereof, that determines the damage incurred.

Do we hear someone asking, "What has all this to do with the context of environmental politics?" Our answer is, "A great deal." The continuing potential, and recurrent actual, shortage of energy provides as good an example as any. For several decades, well-qualified experts have been warning of an approaching energy crisis. But only a tiny minority have paid the slightest attention.[6] Except for a brief period of rationing during World War II, Americans have simply taken for granted that there would always be plenty of cheap motor fuel, heating oil, natural gas, and electric power. They paid no attention to reports of emerging changes that could disrupt their accustomed styles of living. Even responsible public authorities long turned a deaf ear to such expert warnings.[7] In some instances, even those in positions of ready access to expert advice asserted, after the event and contrary to fact, that the fuel shortage was neither foreseen nor foreseeable.[8] In short, discrepancies between subjective images and objective conditions enter at many points into the calculations of policymakers and their constituents and thereby become important ingredients of the context of environmental politics.

Ubiquitous Indeterminacy

As intimated at numerous points in the preceding discussion, an element of indeterminacy lurks in most if not quite all our questions for policymakers. This is so because concerns evoked by diminishing natural resources, environmental pollutions, and disruptions of the biosphere pertain to future innovations or to future consequences of present trends. Such concerns cannot be calculated with certitude because the future cannot be known but only conjectured with varying degrees of credibility. This concluding section is addressed to some of the limitations of futuristic calculations without, however, detouring very far into theories of explanation and prediction.[9]

A great many people are interested in the past. One thinks of the propensity of elderly folk to reminisce. One notes the popularity of memoirs, biographies, topical histories, historical fiction, and historical spectaculars. Academic curricula are loaded with historical subjects. Tradition bulks large in the rituals of churches and other institutions. These and other indicators confirm the pervasive presence of the past.

Most of us behave most of the time as if we anticipate a future that is not very different from the past with which we are familiar. However, interest in the past, and expectation of a future recognizably familiar, do not contradict the observation that living is predominantly oriented toward the future. This orientation is evident in countless minor as well as major decisions: when to cross a busy street, what to serve for dinner, whether to consult a doctor, where to invest one's savings, etc. Without sense of risk of future damage from existing and anticipated conditions in working place and other environments, very little if any protective legislation would be enacted.

Most people appear to recognize—some clearly, most vaguely

—an element of uncertainty in their expectations. Discerning people also recognize that uncertainty is greater in some situations than in others: for example, a great deal more is known about the risk of contracting trichinosis from eating undercooked pork than is known about the human damage that may become evident fifty years hence from scores of nations dumping huge quantities of raw sewage, garbage, industrial residues, and other pollutants into the ocean.

A lengthening interval between exposure and definitive diagnosis is characteristic of a great many contemporary vulnerabilities. It is especially evident in connection with technical innovations. The automobile is a prime exhibit. It took half a century for some of the more harmful impacts of highway motor vehicles to become clearly evident. Lengthening time-lags may help to account for growing demands for earlier identification of risks, despite uncertainties inherent in all futuristic calculations.

Such felt need is evident with regard not only to personal safety and health but also to advance planning in business and government. In 1975, for example, a survey disclosed that officers of utility companies in numerous parts of the country were baffled as well as frustrated by less than predicted demand for electric power. Their frustration derived not only from reduced consumption but also from the shadow that reduction of demand cast over planning. It may take as long as a decade to design, site, finance, construct, and put into operation a contemporary large-capacity plant. If, as there are some rather plausible grounds for surmising, we are in the midst of a radical transition, a process of unknowable duration, characterized by more than a few historic discontinuities, it casts doubt on the relevance of the principles of ceteris paribus and simple linear extrapolation as bases for projecting a more or less uncertain future from a partially known past.

It is axiomatic that no futuristic calculation can rise above the assumptions upon which it is founded. Such assumptions about future conditions are not observed conditions and trends. Hence, futuristic scenarios cannot escape the indeterminacy inherent in a future that has not yet occurred.

Allowing for unavoidable uncertainty, futuristic conjectures by relevant specialists are at least prima facie more credible than those by persons who command less specifically relevant knowledge. With regard to oil reserves, no one knows with certainty what exploratory drilling may yet discover. Even those geologists whose specialty is identification of likely oil-bearing earth structures may reach different estimates. But their judgments on this issue—provided these are not biased by terms of employment or other interests that conflict with professional probity—are presumably more reliable than those, say, of a professional musician. Engineers, likewise, may differ as to how much of the oil underground can be extracted with equipment and skills available or in prospect. But they presumably know more about oil technology than does a professor of rhetoric. Economists may differ regarding the cost of extracting recoverable reserves. But their judgments are prima facie more trustworthy than those derived from viewing television. There is always some uncertainty about constraints imposed by governmental institutions and processes, and by reactions of the public to whom politicians are responsive. But professional students of government seem likely to understand these constraints better than most of their fellow citizens. In short, we are suggesting by these examples that experts—persons with specialized knowledge, skills, and experience—are prima facie more reliable calculators of future possibilities and probabilities, *within the boundaries of their expertise*.

Speaking generally, and with allowance for qualifications, it is a misuse of such experts for legislatures, litigants, businessmen, journalists, or others to demand (as they repeatedly do) a degree of certainty that exceeds existing knowledge. It is an even worse misuse of experts to try to shift onto them the policy choices and decisions that are the responsibility of business managements and political executives and legislators.[10]

In many contexts, however, public authorities, businessmen, and concerned citizens in general need something in addition to a collection of specialized judgments. This something additional is integration of such judgments into futuristic syntheses, or scenarios, that embody interrelations of a few or many variables, as the case may be. Such syntheses should contribute to better understanding of all systems, especially living systems—about which, more in the next chapter.

In many instances, the fact of damage is well established: for example, the prevalence of lung disease among long-term coal miners. An essential precondition of effective protection against this affliction is determination of its cause. This is obviously a question for expert assessment. If the verdict is, let us say, prolonged exposure to dust-laden air in poorly ventilated mines, the next question is: What *can* be done about it? This question, too, calls for expert advice, especially if alternative corrective solutions are available. Then comes the question: What will the job cost?—another matter for expert assessment. Finally comes the question: What *should* be done? This question, unlike the preceding ones, involves a *political* decision. That is, it involves considerations of public interest, moral duty, sense of urgency, priorities among competing claims, and resources available, as well as probable effectiveness and cost of alternative options: in short, it involves a composite judgment in the ethically tangled context of legislative politics.

Many of the major issues of environmental politics present baffling uncertainties. Consider, for example, the disputed issue of the effects of atmospheric pollution from many sources, not in the microenvironment of a coal mine but in the macroenvironment of a large country, larger region, or the earth as a whole. Polluted air in such an environment may contain a complex mixture of more or less toxic substances. Much has yet to be learned regarding the effects of different pollutants on health. Furthermore, people may vary in their tolerance of respiratory irritants. Physiological tolerances vary not only with age and general health, but also with intensity and duration of exposure. In view of these and other uncertainties, is it preferable to treat the symptoms of those injured, or alternatively to apply the incomplete knowledge available to reducing the sources of injury? Either course bristles with technical issues regarding which reasonable persons may disagree. For example, it may be as difficult to refute as to substantiate claims that any effective action is likely to disrupt industries, destroy jobs, erode profits, raise consumer prices, and produce still other politically unwanted consequences. Such uncertainties can be narrowed but rarely eliminated from the subjective calculus of political decisions.

Any serious attempt to evaluate conflicting predictions involves analysis and calculations of complex interactions among clusters of conditions that are changing at different rates in different places. Yet the human future may well depend on the quality of such integrative calculations, and on authoritative decisions based thereon.

A fair exhibit of the uncertainties as well as complexities in such systemic calculations is the "limits to growth" model that evoked a storm of angry and some vituperative criticism in the early 1970s.[11] The architects of that model, after extensive research and cogitation, decided that the factors most likely to shape the human future during the next century could be grouped into five clusters: national and global rates of population growth, industrial development and production, food production, depletion of nonrenewable resources, and environmental pollutions. With regard to each cluster, a good deal is known about current conditions and trends, though many of the data are more or less unreliable. Future trends within each cluster of variables present many uncertainties; and interactions among various combinations of these factors entail a considerable element of conjecture.

Now let us see how these indeterminacies were handled. Reports of the research team reflect critical assessment of available data, and a range of assumptions (including conservative ones) regarding changes and interactions among the five clusters chosen. By combining these different assumptions into numerous hypothetical permutations, the researchers derived a number of possible patterns of future developments. From these calculations, they drew the following general conclusion:

"If present growth trends in world population, industrialization, pollution, food production, and resource depletion continue unchanged, the limits to growth . . . will be reached sometime within the next one hundred years. The most probable result will be a rather sudden and uncontrollable decline in both population and industrial capacity."[12]

Note that the authors did not assert that the stated collateral conditions, from which they deduced this conclusion, would certainly or necessarily continue unchanged. Nor did they predict dogmatically that the calculated disasters would in fact occur. They explained their reasons for choosing the five clusters of variables and described their calculations regarding the future interactions of those variables. From these calculations, they deduced certain specific conclusions, presumably valid only if the specified trends do in fact "continue unchanged." They did not assert that these conditions would continue unchanged. On the contrary, they were specific in suggesting policy decisions—domestic, foreign, international—that would probably avoid the disasters deduced from unchanged trends.

Throughout the project, if one believes that the authors did what they report (and we see no plausible ground for doubt), the "limits to growth" model reflects generally accepted canons of explanation and prediction. The authors adhered to the formula: If specified conditions *A, B . . . N* prevail, then *X* will occur, or will probably occur. They made all this explicit, leaving little or no tenable ground for accusing them of bootlegging dogmatic forecasts in through some cellar window. Their conclusion was a contingent prediction—that is, contingent on certain specified assumptions regarding future conditions. Whether these conditions develop as assumed will depend, in part, on political decisions, about which much uncertainty exists, as well as on changes in the milieu from other factors than such decisions.

One might legitimately criticize their choice of critically significant factors. One might contend that they failed to consider sufficiently some of the factors likely to influence decisions that would alter their projected trends: in particular, differences among political systems and the forces to which public authorities are likely to be responsive. But, we repeat, no one could fairly accuse them (as numerous critics did) of dogmatically predicting that specified possible outcomes would actually or necessarily occur. Indeed, in essential respects, their procedures were identical, or at least remarkably similar, to those employed by some of their severe critics.

"Limits to growth" and other futuristic scenarios are not predictions of a future entirely beyond human control. Futuristic conjectures are sometimes expressed in dogmatic, even deterministic, rhetoric. But genuine environmental determinists are a rare if not extinct species. Deterministic rhetoric, however, is a ubiquitous weapon in environmental discussion. It may be employed to warn people to change their ways before it is too late to matter, or to enlist their support for some hypothetical utopia, or to buttress defense of a weak cause. Hence the importance of critically inspecting the assumptions upon which all futuristic conjectures are founded. For example, if the scenario architect assumes that scientific and engineering research will sustain economic growth indefinitely, his scenario will differ radically from the "limits to growth" models.

Such comparisons reveal differences in presuppositions about nature and in other determinants of futuristic speculation. That is to say, comparison of futuristic scenarios discloses conflicting philosophical postures. These differences in posture help to account for disputations over strategies and priorities at the heart of environmental policymaking and hence deserve further consideration in this exploration of the context of environmental politics.

Conflicting Philosophical Postures

PHILOSOPHICAL postures deserve more attention than they generally receive in discussions of environmental policymaking. They penetrate to the core of environmental politics, affecting decisions regarding what *should* be undertaken toward decelerating the destructive exploitation of nature and arresting disruptive impacts on systems that sustain life upon the earth.

By philosophical posture, we mean a person's image of the world, and of his relation to it. Philosophical posture is revealed in attitudes, perspectives, and ethical codes. By attitude we mean simply a person's mental state or inclination toward an object or state of affairs. Perspective: in the metaphor of photography, the location of the camera, the objects toward which it is pointed, and the breadth of the field from which the lens transmits data to the sensitized film. Ethical code: a set of moral principles or guiding beliefs; in the aggregate, a person's or a society's ethos.

Postures toward the earth and its inhabitants, human as well as nonhuman, can be compared in various ways. The way selected here is to compare the extent to which they exhibit exploitive and mutualistic qualities. A maximally exploitive attitude would be one that envisages inert matter, nonhuman species, and even humans as objects to be possessed or manipulated to suit the purposes of the exploiter. In contrast, a maximally mutualistic posture would be one that emphasizes the interrelatedness of things and manifests a preference for cooperation and accommodation rather than conflict and domination.

It would be naïve to pretend that many people, if any at all, fit neatly into one or another philosophical posture. For example, a politician may condemn lying in principle, but practice it when truth conflicts with his loyalty to leader or party. A merchant may be candid and generous within his family circle, but in his business "let the buyer beware." Such behavioral contradictions, however, do not diminish the importance of philosophical postures which, like prisms, shape one's images of reality, and thereby influence responses thereto.

The thesis of this chapter is that debates over conditions and changes in the earth's life-supportive habitat, and over what should be done to protect both habitat and inhabitants, reveal and are affected by postures that are respectively more exploitive than mutualistic or more mutualistic than exploitive.

Exploitation Predominant

Philosophical postures that are predominantly exploitive appear in various contexts and under different labels. Such postures show up in interpersonal relations and in attitudes toward nonhuman nature. Implicit, sometimes explicit, is the presumption that nature is simply potential plunder to be seized and consumed: "Since man is the highest creature, all nature must have been created for him." This hoary teleological pretense has been attributed to Judeo-Christian metaphysics, to the development of empirical science, and to various other sources. It was summed up by the American geographer Isaiah Bowman, in two caustic sentences: "Most men take the view that the world is their oyster. They are out for conquest."[1]

Singleness of purpose is a characteristic feature of this posture. In academic and industrial research, business practices, many governmental operations, and other contexts, this characteristic is manifest in preoccupation with a specific task in hand: how to build a more lethal missile; how to contain a recurrently flooding river; how to increase the annual wheat crop; how to cure currently incurable diseases: in short, how to achieve some specific objective.

Singleness of purpose encourages a way of perceiving that is sometimes called tunnel vision. This metaphor emphasizes that minimal attention, or none at all, is given to possibly harmful collateral consequences (by-products, side effects) of the project in hand. More powerful automobiles have been built, with scant regard for their effects on fuel consumption and human safety. Larger crop yields have been achieved by massive applications of nitrates and phosphates, with no anticipation of harmful seepage into watercourses and aquifers. Synthetic products of many kinds—plastics, nylon, detergents, and many others—have been invented and put on the market with little or no investigation of their effects on the consumers or their physical surroundings.

One could continue almost indefinitely, citing examples of tunnel vision—a way of perceiving (to change the metaphor) analogous to photographing a vast and varied landscape through a narrow-angle lens covered with a filter that blocks out all colors but one. If harmful effects should subsequently occur, the exploiters confidently assume that ways can be invented to cope. Faith in the remedial magic of applied science provides a prudence-dulling rationale for taking technological risks, even major leaps into relatively unexplored frontiers.

Willingness, even enthusiasm, for taking such risks is evident in expanding research agendas for recombining the genetic building blocks of life. Something similar is implicit in the so called Faustian bargain, which receives further attention in the next chapter. Here it is sufficient to note that risk-taking has penetrated deeply into the subculture of science.

Conflicting philosophical postures come sharply into focus in disputations over the social responsibilities of scientists, inventors, and entrepreneurs. Previous to the 1940s, many innovations produced harmful consequences: for example, introduction of rapid-firing guns and poisonous gases to improve the art of killing people. But none of these earlier innovations approached the potential for environmental destruction and human slaughter that followed the breakthrough in nuclear physics and subsequent applications to weaponry and, more recently, to generation of electric power.

This abrupt historical discontinuity is part of the setting against which the social responsibility of scientists has begun to receive more serious consideration. Some have disavowed any responsibility at all. Fairly typical, we submit (as of the early 1970s, at least), was the response of an aerospace physicist to the question whether he had given serious thought to the social implications of allocating billions to put a few men upon the moon, when a small fraction of that outlay could have made a sizable dent in the hunger that still pervades even the world's most affluent society. His response: "No; why should I?"

More recently a committee of the American Association for the Advancement of Science has documented this indifference. The committee also reports numerous instances of governmental and private employers rewarding scientific employees for silence, and harassing or discharging those who publicly reveal hazards in materials and processes marketed by their employers. The report cites cases involving lax standards for exposure to radiation, to industrial chemicals, and to numerous other hazards.

Commenting on the long silence of physicians employed by companies mining and processing asbestos and other hazardous materials, the committee concluded that those medical experts were guilty of "abdication of . . . responsibility"—but added in extenuation: "Obviously a doctor who is paid by a commercial enterprise will find it very difficult to act contrary to the policy of the company. . . . We [also] know from experience that regulatory agencies [of government] often become the subservient allies of the organizations that they are supposed to regulate and may collaborate . . . in concealing the hazards."[2]

The issue of responsibility surfaced again at the 1976 annual convention of the AAAS. In a panel discussion, a major corporation's vice-president for research asserted that the industrial scientist "owes loyalty to his employer." If he is unwilling to accept this constraint, he should "be willing to resign."[3]

Whether this is the generally prevailing view of business managements, we do not pretend to know. But we note that, with rare exceptions, in controversies over the hazards of chemical reagents, synthetic consumer goods, and various other products, industrial scientists side publicly with their employers —or keep still.

The question of social responsibility is emerging today in a still broader context. The traditional position of most scientists is that research agendas should be determined by those who do the research. Emphasizing this posture, the chairman of the biology department of a leading university says: "Some of my colleagues feel that it is the scientist's job to do science, and society's job to cope with what he does."[4]

Implicit in this claim are, first, the dubious assumption that "pure science" is in fact ethically neutral, and second, the morally contestable assertion that responsibility for the social and environmental consequences of science-based innovations should rest entirely upon the businessmen and others who gain from the innovation in question. Furthermore, these positions implicitly exclude a great many nonscientists—probably most of the readers of this book—from any effective opportunity to influence decisions that may vitally affect them.

This civic consequence has evoked numerous reactions. One critic queries the moral propriety of "involved scientists closeted with financially interested industrialists and governmental authorities" going ahead without effective precautions. Scientific and engineering decisions that may entail major social consequences, especially very adverse ones, should include "members of the general public after hearing all sides of the questions, with balanced inputs from scientists, humanists, historians, philosophers, theologians, and, most of all, from ordinary citizens."[5]

This position acquires additional significance from predicted hazards of recombinant DNA research. Commenting on this burgeoning field, a member of the editorial staff of *Science* (published by the AAAS) emphasizes that such research "will clearly bring to birth a technology so potent that even its slightest deviations from the intended path may cause grievous perturbations in society at large." This follows from the premise that ability to recombine genes "is the beginning of the genetic engineering of bacteria, of plants and domestic animals, and ultimately of man."[6]

During half a century in academia, we have known many scientists and research engineers. Some of them clearly have tried to exclude ethical norms from their professional work. Others seem to be motivated by norms more appropriate to the marketplace than to academic seminars and laboratories. We have known still others who expressed concern regarding the social and environmental consequences of their research. The overall picture of the ethical inputs of scientific research is by no means clear and cannot be resolved here.

Minimal recognition of social responsibility has long characterized entrepreneurial behavior. It continues to appear in utterances and practices of business managements and business-linked publications. It is not unknown for businessmen to deny such responsibility altogether, insisting that their paramount responsibility is to maximize profits for their shareholders as well as for themselves.[7]

We do not find this posture surprising. The premises of private-enterprise economics predispose business managements (with occasional exceptions) toward short-term gains. This posture also conditions them to resist restrictive regulations imposed by public authority and to oppose centrally planned distribution of income and wealth. Business managements (again, with exceptions) have clung tenaciously to some of the most exploitive doctrines of classical economics, embedded in practice and sanctified in historic principles of the common law.

However, there are exceptions, as noted above; and these include businessmen with unimpeachable private-enterprise credentials. For example, at a conference in 1976, the chairman of a metropolitan bank was reported to have said that "the market, essential as it is, is myopic; it is good for dealing with problems that lie only five or seven or possibly ten years ahead, but our most serious problems are long-range problems."[8]

A public relations entrepreneur warns the business and financial communities that their traditional civic posture not only gives ammunition to their critics, but could wreck our relatively free private enterprise system.[9]

These cautionary warnings, to which others could be added, do not necessarily indicate a trend. So far as we can discover, slowly spreading awareness of personal and societal damage and hazards associated with conditions and changes in the physical environment have yet to show much impact on the practices and policies that issue from industrial corporations, numerous governmental agencies, and other influential niches in our society.[10]

A predominantly exploitive posture is usually, though not invariably, associated with a strongly materialistic ethos. This association is conspicuous in attitudes toward the gross national product (GNP). Strictly speaking, GNP is simply a statistical concept denoting the total quantity of money paid for goods and services within a given economy in a given year. As such, GNP comes close to being ethically neutral.

However, the symbol GNP has acquired strong ethical overtones. A rising GNP is almost universally conceived to be ipso facto an unqualified "good," a goal of high priority. To the question How much is enough? most Americans will answer: More and more, ad infinitum—an answer buttressed by marketplace economics.

Leaving aside the question of how long this style of economic growth can continue, critics emphasize that the ingredients of GNP, as generally conceived, include a great deal that is only marginally "good" or not "good" at all. Items mentioned in the latter category include monies paid for grossly wasteful consumption of energy and materials, endlessly expanding stockpiles of military hardware, and expenditures for ostentatious luxuries. All such items are included in statistics of GNP.

Defenders of current-style economic growth retort that only by expanding the GNP will it ever become possible to cover proliferating social and environmental demands. They also claim that harmful side effects from expanding production in more and more countries need cause no alarm. They express confidence that scientists and engineers, financed by business and government, will invent adequate substitutes for dwindling high-grade natural materials and will tap abundant new sources of energy, as well as keep within tolerable limits the pollutions and other sources of vulnerability incidental to economic growth. One also hears it contended that the risk of rendering the earth progressively less fit for human habitation is too speculative, and the hazards, if any, too remote, to justify curtailing or redirecting growth *now*. As one economist puts it, "To stop growing now . . . would be to commit suicide for fear of remote death."[11]

Those who envision social reform and environmental repair and protection to be feasible only as by-products of expanding production seem reluctant, as a rule, to contemplate major changes in the existing distribution of income, wealth, privilege, and power. They rarely give much consideration to the possibility that more adequate protection for the domestic society and its habitat could be financed, in some part, by rationalizing the military budget, by refusing to approve more superhighways and other environmentally destructive projects, and by reducing wasteful consumption of energy in industry, transport, and so on.

Arguments over budgetary priorities often appear to reflect an assumption that continued rapid growth with a perpetually expanding GNP is the only acceptable solution—that is, the only solution that does not seriously disturb the amenities and luxuries of the already well-to-do. Implicit, only rarely explicit, in this posture is the sanctity of the status quo buttressed by an ethos that justifies nearly any change except substantial redistribution of income and wealth.

One rarely hears it argued publicly these days that what is good for the rich is ipso facto good for the poor, by a trickling down of prosperity through the industrial-social hierarchy. But some such ethos lurks between the lines in much of the continuing disputation over strategies for reducing discrimination, poverty, and destitution. It is a tenet of marketplace economics that workers are merely components of the productive process—robots on an assembly line, statistical items in corporate accounts, numbers fed into a computer, valuable chiefly as they contribute to production of goods and services.[12] Some such principle follows logically from the exploitive posture that has informed much of the thinking and doing along the road of rising affluence achieved at the price of wasteful expenditure of energy and materials as well as exploitation of human resources and progressive disruption of the biosphere.

Most economists, we anticipate, will reject these comments on their discipline's ethical premises. Many, we repeat, will counter that economic growth is the most promising, if not the only, escape route from the dilemma of increasing population, proliferating demands, and insufficient disposable goods and services. Some will deny that our finite habitat imposes any unpierceable ceiling on current-style growth within any future that they consider relevant. A few envision even accelerative rates of growth in an increasing number of countries as the less developed countries (LDCs) strive to emulate the industrial giants —an issue to which we return in chapter 6.

We recognize that many able scholars sincerely share these expectations. But for others, ourselves included, this hubristic optimism evokes many questions. How can anyone be confident that technological innovations and the marketplace can overcome or circumvent the obstacles implicit in dwindling reserves of high-grade natural materials? Or prevent worsening pollutions of air, water, and land? Or reduce sufficiently the risk of disrupting the complex biotic systems that sustain life upon our finite planet? Does the prescription of endless current-style economic growth take sufficient account of the *political* as well as technical obstacles to be overcome? Do prevailing images of the social-political milieu perhaps underestimate the multiplicity and political muscle of competing claimants for larger shares of the national income? Can the essential values of industrial society be attained by a process less environmentally destructive than those that have widely prevailed to date?

Some politicians, economists, and businessmen have put so

many eggs into the basket of long-term, forced-draft, current-style growth that it is difficult to envision what alternative strategies they might opt for if the eggs fail to hatch, or if the hatched chicks fail to survive—or, to change the metaphor, if events should demonstrate that their time-honored prescription simply will not cure the disease.[13]

Not all economists subscribe to the orthodoxy of indefinite economic expansion. An apparently increasing number are giving serious consideration to the limits of our finite earth and to the damage and hazards implicit in the growth process as hitherto defined and defended. We shall return to their critiques, with special reference to short-term energy supplies and long-term hazards in the next and later chapters.[14]

We conclude this section with a reminder that an exploitive posture toward nature, and commitment to salvation by innovative technology and economic growth, are by no means confined to societies founded upon private-enterprise capitalism. The practices associated with this posture are reported to be just as pervasive in authoritarian, centrally planned politico-economic systems—and for essentially similar reasons. One specialist on Soviet economics says: "If the study of environmental disruption in the Soviet Union demonstrates anything, it shows that not private enterprise but industrialization is the primary cause of environmental disruption."[15]

Mutualistic Challenge

The exploitive posture, and the ethos by which it is rationalized and sustained, have not gone unchallenged. In chapter 1, we reviewed briefly the weak and largely ineffective, but persistent, protests against disruptive plundering of the earth. Today's challengers include traditional conservationists, professional ecologists, amateur naturalists, along with geographers, demographers, economists, and critics from numerous other backgrounds. Initiatives have come from all of these sources, but especially from ecologists. They have supplied much of the rationale and some of the evidence that associate damage and hazards with activities that wastefully deplete, poisonously pollute, and otherwise degrade the biosphere. For this reason in particular, but also because there is so much misconception regarding ecological science, we have elected to summarize here the philosophical posture and our conception of some of the premises and theories that ecologists have contributed to the context of environmental politics.

Before doing so, we should emphasize explicitly that this book is not a treatise on ecology, and that we are not professional ecologists. However, we have borrowed extensively from the substance and vocabulary of ecological theory which has contributed more perhaps than any other system of knowledge to understanding of the consequences of progressive spoliation of the earth and disruption of natural systems.

As intimated above, few terms are more misused than ecology and ecologist. For some, ecology means simply preserving the remnants of primeval nature. For others, the essence of ecology is nothing more than abatement of pollutions. For others, ecology and ecologist have become pejorative epithets. For numerous social activists, ecology stands for diversion of scarce resources from more urgent "human" needs. Since about the mid-1960s, ecology has become a fad-word used loosely and indiscriminately. Many well-educated people appear to imagine environmental relationships to be the total substance of ecology. It is true that ecologists dwell on nature's impacts on humans, and vice versa. But such relationships are no more the sum total of ecology than a dog's head is a dog.

Ecology is a science in the same sense that physics and economics are sciences. The designative label of any science identifies a system of interrelated presuppositions, data, models, and theories that purport to describe what and how things happen and are likely to happen within the segment of reality on which the particular science is focused. Moreover, like all scientists, ecologists live in two worlds: on the one hand, the world of more or less objective observation, analysis, description, projection, and creative theorizing; on the other, the world of civic identification and subjective notions of what is desirable and undesirable, what is good and bad in an ethical sense. We emphasize this objective/subjective dualism because these two worlds impinge on each other in the personality of every scientist—physicist, biologist, economist, ecologist, or whatever—and sometimes these two worlds are in conflict with one another.

Most contemporary ecologists started as biologists. Many ecological concepts, some of the theories, and the vocabulary in which they are often expressed reflect this professional background. Until well into the present century, ecologists concentrated almost exclusively on nonhuman populations and habitats. Broadly speaking, ecological research was directed primarily toward learning how particular mixtures of plants and animals coexist within a given geographic habitat, and how some biotic communities, or certain species within such a community, thrive and survive while others languish and perish.

Concepts of plant and animal ecology began to filter into the study of human communities early in this century.[16] However, most professional ecologists continued to concentrate on nonhuman ecosystems. Only within the last generation or so have any substantial number enlarged their focus to include human communities and social systems. In the course of adaptation, a somewhat different science is emerging, derived from but not identical with the ecology of fifty or more years ago. Ecologists have described in various ways what has happened.

According to Paul Sears, human-inclusive ecology "is a study of the entire ecosystem. Of this system man is not just an observer and irresponsible exploiter but an integral part, now the world's dominant organism."[17]

Barry Commoner has described this derivative, human-oriented ecology as "the science of planetary housekeeping." Still a "young science," it has yet to achieve "the kind of cohesive, simplifying generalizations exemplified by, say, the laws of physics." However, Commoner suggests four generalizations which he calls "informal . . . laws of ecology": (1) "Everything is connected to everything else"; (2) "Everything must go somewhere"; (3) "Any major man-made change in a natural system is likely to be detrimental to that system"; and (4) "There is no such thing as a free lunch."[18]

Others (including some not professionally identified with ecological science) might suggest at least two additional generalizations: (5) Human survival depends upon certain conditions that (so far as is known today) exist only upon the planet earth; and (6) Except for energy received from the sun, the planet earth is a closed system—that is, a finite habitat incapable of sustaining indefinitely a globally increasing population currently doubling every thirty to thirty-five years.[19]

As we understand it the basic model of ecological science is derived from generalization 5 above. Reduced to bare essentials, with many details and qualifications omitted and thus with some risk of misconception, this model can be summarized as follows: Plants receive energy transmitted from the sun and transmute some of this energy by a complex biochemical process called photosynthesis into compounds of carbon and hydrogen. This process releases free oxygen and converts lifeless matter into nutrients that sustain plants and provide food for animals that consume plants, and indirectly for animals that consume other animals. All these organisms (plants and animals) eventually die and are decomposed by microorganisms that transform dead tissues into compounds that return to the pool of nutrients that is also simultaneously enriched by continuing photosynthesis that sustains other plants and animals; in this way the "web of life" continues.[20]

The energy that has kept this system going comes from the sun, either via continuing photosynthesis as indicated above, or as heat absorbed by organisms and inert matter, or as power transmitted by moving air and water or stored in geothermal reservoirs or in fossil fuels.

Hypothetically, the life processes in the biosphere can continue indefinitely, provided certain necessary conditions prevail. One of these is that enough but not too much solar energy continues to be received upon the earth's surface. Another is that changes in the terrestrial biosphere, either from phenomena of nature or from human activities, or from both in interaction, do not irreparably disrupt the web of life.

Disruptive changes in solar output could be either gradual and insidious or abrupt and cataclysmic. A contingency of another type is the accelerative depletion of stored energy, especially petroleum and natural gas. Still another possibility is that piecemeal cumulative contamination of the oceans by garbage, sewage, industrial effluents, spilled oil, and other residues of human activities may eventually disrupt the vital process of photosynthesis there where so much of it occurs. Irreparable disruption of this process, it is conjectured, could break the food chain and hence disrupt the web of life at its terrestrial source. In short, speaking metaphorically, the biotic clock would simply run down.

Another cluster of possibilities, closely related to those listed above, is that continued population increase at the current, or even a substantially lower, rate will further accelerate denudation and disruption of the biosphere. In this case the biotic clock will run down sooner.

The possibility of abrupt nuclear catastrophe has been endlessly debated ever since the invention of nuclear weapons. Many qualified scientists and informed laymen are convinced that large-scale warfare conducted with such weapons could contaminate air, water, land, nonhuman organisms, and human bodies on a scale sufficient to render much or all of the earth uninhabitable within a short time. However, nuclear warfare has received relatively little attention in the continuing discussions of environmental crisis, even though it is one of the focal points in the setting of environmental politics, to which we shall give further attention in chapter 6.

Terminal or nearly terminal catastrophe from these or numerous other sources may or may not be as imminent as some scientists have contended. Such a catastrophe may not occur at all. Nevertheless, warnings from qualified experts serve a useful purpose. These warnings draw attention to the kinds of disruptive changes that already are seriously disturbing the conditions upon which civilization, and possibly all life upon the earth, depend.

It is the magnitude and rate of disruptive changes as much as the conjectural possibility of their terminating in irreversible catastrophe within a century more or less that serve notice that humankind are already deeply mired in a dangerous and worsening process of environmental degeneration.

A corollary of the web-of-life model is the linkage of living organisms (including humans) to the earth. A few avant-garde physicists reject this corollary. They assert the technical feasibility of liberating some fraction of humankind from bondage to the earth. They claim that it will be technically possible within a few years or decades to establish self-sustaining colonies in man-made satellites or elsewhere in outer space.

We claim no competence to judge the technical feasibility of such projects. However, for reasons previewed in chapter 1 and to be elaborated in chapters 4 and 8, all projects for escaping the tightening bind of expanding population, dwindling natural resources, and worsening pollutions by emigrating to outer space, seem to us *politically* irrelevant and improbable, regardless of their possible technical feasibility.

So far as we can discover, no life scientist envisions such an escape-hatch from a depleted and disrupted earth. Dubos tells why: "Wherever he goes and whatever he does . . . man must maintain around himself a microenvironment similar to the one under which he evolved . . . as if he remained linked to the our face of the earth by an umbilical cord. He may engage in casual flirtations with nonterrestrial worlds, but he is wedded to the earth, the sole source of sustenance." [21]

If one accepts this judgment (and we see no grounds for rejecting it), then it must follow that the fate of our species as well as the quality of human life will continue to depend upon certain elemental requisites that exist, so far as yet known, only upon the earth. That is the essence of generalization 5, suggested above as a supplement to the four suggested by Commoner.

Dependence not only upon the physical earth—land, water, air—but also upon other forms of terrestrial life—plants, animals, microbes, etc.—and upon the effects of changes in these elements, is the essence of Commoner's first "informal law of ecology": that "everything is connected to everything else."

This is one of the points where ecological science collides head-on with the counterclaim by a few physical scientists that even if humankind is presently tied to the earth, future scientific advances are likely to free humans from this dependence. Such was the prediction, for example, by the late Eugene Rabino-witch. In 1972, in a cheery article full of hubris, he said in part: "The only animals whose disappearance may threaten the biological viability of man on earth are the bacteria normally inhabiting our bodies. For the rest, there is no convincing proof that mankind could not survive as the only animal species on earth. . . . Man may even be able to become independent of plants, on which he now depends as sources of his food." [22]

One may question whether in the present state of knowledge anyone can prove or refute Commoner's hypothesis that "everything is connected to everything else." But it is demonstrable that a great many more things are interrelated than generally recognized and taken into account in the management of human affairs. Moreover, a presumption of universal interrelatedness, whether presently confirmable or not, focuses attention on the multiplicity of collateral consequences identifiable in all large undertakings and in many smaller ones too. The economist Barbara Ward says: "These interdependent aspects of Nature are, in essence, what ecology is all about." [23] The biologist Garrett Hardin emphasizes the same point in his often quoted maxim—"we can never do merely one thing"—a proposition he calls the "fundamental principle of ecology." [24]

Pollutions of air, water, and land exemplify Commoner's second "law": that "everything must go somewhere." A corollary of that proposition is that where things go, and in what form and quantity, determines whether the disposal will produce significantly harmful consequences for safety, health, and other values. Another corollary is that the larger the economic output and the higher the rate of obsolescence, the greater becomes the quantity of residues, safe disposal of which becomes increasingly difficult as well as expensive.

Commoner's third "law-like generalization" that "any major man-made change in a natural system is likely to be detrimental to that system" may or may not be as universal as he suggests. Whether it is or not, it directs attention to disruptive damage that human activities have already inflicted on nature, and on the reciprocal kickbacks suffered in consequence.

Commoner's fourth generalization—that "there is no such thing as a free lunch"—is a proposition on which ecological and economic sciences seem to approach agreement. But this consensus is of recent origin and represents a retreat from the former economic doctrine of free air and a few other things. That classical doctrine long pervaded the teaching of economics. For example, Taussig's *Principles,* from which our generation studied economics in the 1920s, taught that "fresh air, climate, sunshine are obvious cases of free goods." Other texts, then and later, reiterated the gratuitous gifts of nature, denying implicitly the principle of no free lunch. [25]

If ecology and economics appear to be in substantial agreement today on the "free lunch" issue, we repeat that they are still far apart on another: namely, the potential of pure and applied physical science to supplant natural systems. Because numerous ecologists are extremely skeptical about this claim, they are sometimes accused of being hostile to material progress in general, and in particular to the physical sciences that have made much of this progress possible.

Such criticism seems to indicate failure to understand the nature of ecology. So far as we can determine, very few if any professional ecologists are hostile to physical science and science-based engineering. Ecological criticism is directed rather against the propensity of those who command the powerful instruments of contemporary engineering to forge ahead with insufficient attention to, concern for, and calculation of, possibly harmful side effects of undertakings that may seem at first glance to be reasonably safe as well as beneficial. In short, so far as we can discover, ecologists reject not innovative engineering and the science upon which it is based, but disregard of interrelatedness, and the hazards that such disregard entails. What is demanded is not less innovation but more concern for and better comprehension of the possibly harmful consequences of technological sorties into unknown or only partly reconnoitered landscapes.

So far as we are aware, no professional ecologist pretends to a full understanding of all the living systems that are relevant to human well-being and long-term survival. However, more is being learned about these systemic relationships, and by methods more or less common to all empirical sciences, including those whose practitioners are among the severe critics of ecological science.[26]

Some concept of complex system is central to ecological science. A corollary of this concept is a bias against exclusive reliance on analytic reductionism—the propensity in many sciences (physical, biological, social) to shift analysis from complex wholes toward constituent elements thereof. One could cite many objections to excessive reductionism in ecology, but a few samples will suffice.

Dubos (biologist): "When life is considered only in its specialized functions, the outcome is a world emptied of meaning."

Ward (economist): "For each stone flung violently into the pond, there are widening circles of disturbance, and as the stone grows larger and the pond does not increase, the impact becomes more severe and potentially more damaging. These interdependent aspects of Nature are, in essence, what ecology is all about."

Schumacher (economist) chides other economists for failure to take account of the "total situation," the separate elements of which are "not separately predictable, since the parts cannot be understood unless the whole is understood."

Odum (biologist): "Going beyond reductionism to holism is

now mandated if science and society are to mesh for mutual benefit. . . . [Not only ecology but all sciences] must emerge into new hitherto unrecognized and unresearched levels of thinking and action."

Commoner sums it up in a single sentence: a complex living system cannot be understood "simply by looking at the properties of its isolated parts."[27]

Limitations of a narrow field of vision are strikingly evident in the context of multiple vulnerabilities that compete for insufficient disposable resources. A systemic approach directs attention, for example, to the preemptive financial constraint of long-term commitments. A commitment, say, to a ten-year highway-building program not only produces easily discernible changes in the physical landscape, it also locks up revenues that otherwise might become available for better protection of the social and physical environments. Advance commitment of resources is increasing in nearly every sector of governmental activity and has a direct bearing on the fate of environmental programs. This is one of our principal reasons for insisting that the discussion of environmental repair and protection be put and kept within the larger context of the total politics of the society and of the inchoate world community.

It is sometimes countered that holistic and reductionist methods are mutually exclusive and incompatible. We see no reason why this should be so. These are rather complementary ways of investigating reality. Emphasis on "seeing things whole" is analogous to urging people to look at the forest instead of merely individual trees. It is the opposite of the posture ascribed to a well-known politician, regarding conservation of at least some of the great redwood forests: "When you have seen one tree, you have seen them all."

Seeing the forest whole does not guarantee that different viewers will "see" exactly the same whole. However, it does emphasize a "way of seeing" that directs attention to the interrelatedness linking individuals and communities not only to one another but also to nonhuman nature.[28]

Anthropocentricity—and Other Centricities

From the foregoing sketches of philosophical postures designated exploitive and mutualistic, one might conclude that only the former is inherently anthropocentric—that is, assigns highest priority to human wants. That is not the message that we are trying to convey. Exploitive and mutualistic postures exhibit a core of normative agreement: that human values do and should take precedence over others.

One finds, it is true, a few apparent contradictions. For example, one ecologist has deplored the "one species fixation" of so many environmental activists. There can be no "ecology of human survival without the survival of thousands of species . . . on their own terms."[29]

This statement and similar ones by other ecologists, read in context, do not claim parity among all species. What we understand them to claim is rather that the human condition and prospect would be brighter if human relations with nonhuman nature were more symbiotic and less parasitical.

Eugene Odum states this thesis explicitly: "Man thrives best when he functions as part of Nature rather than as a separate unit that strives only to exploit Nature for his immediate needs or temporary gain (as might a newly acquired parasite). Since man is a dependent heterotroph [that is, he feeds on other organisms], he must learn to live in mutualism with Nature; otherwise, like the 'unwise' parasite, he may so exploit his 'host' that he destroys himself."[30]

With the exception of a few strict vegetarians, even those who avow mutualism with nature do not reject food of animal origin. When a wet season brings a plague of mosquitoes, even tough defenders of wildlife accept (perhaps grudgingly) resort to chemical insecticides to prevent encephalitis, malaria, and other insect-borne diseases. In addition to exploiting plants and animals for food, and even destroying wildlife if this is judged necessary to protect human life, dedicated nature conservationists acquiesce (by acts if not words) in the depletion of nonhuman nature in numerous other ways, such as by burning fossil fuels, which once burned are gone forever. They may cherish amenities made from nonrenewable natural materials. They may drive automobiles that pollute the atmosphere. Some defend overcropping, depletive fishing, and other degradations of nature as at least temporary expedients to sustain a human population doubling every thirty to thirty-five years.

For reasons such as these, philosophical postures designated *exploitive* and *mutualistic* identify relative emphases rather than absolute differences. However, we are *not* suggesting that this core of apparent normative agreement diminishes the importance of the distinction between explicitly exploitive and avowedly mutualistic postures. The significance of the distinction emerges as soon as one looks beyond generalities to this question: What rate and intensity of technically possible exploitation is also ethically defensible? The question cannot be answered by benefit-cost formulas. But the question nevertheless lurks in all discussions of "acceptable environmental quality." When one translates acceptability into specific activities to be permitted or prohibited and specific damage and hazards to be tolerated, important differences in ethical standards quickly emerge.

If one views the earth as plunder to be possessed and consumed at rates that maximize short-term gains, it is manifestly a short step to the position that the earth and its nonhuman populations were created expressly for homo sapiens to exploit to suit his purposes, whatever these may be. From such an ethos, it is another short step to the myopic attitude that justifies any kind and rate of exploitation, regardless not only of current damage but also of continuing hazards that will be passed along to future generations.

If, in contrast, the earth is perceived not as exploitable plunder, but rather as an estate in trust, to be prudently managed and then bequeathed to posterity in as viable condition as possible, a decidedly different ethical coloration is given to practices that needlessly deplete and disrupt the estate for the short-term benefit of the present temporary tenants without concern for the longer-range future.[31]

Until elemental needs, especially food, are reasonably assured, the struggle for subsistence is likely to blot out concern for a more distant future. Perpetually hungry people rarely exhibit much empathy toward, or mutualism with, nature. What is more noteworthy is the pervasiveness of "take-all-you-can-get-*now*" among people whose essential needs are well assured. To the question What does such an egocentric posture imply for future generations? a great many in our midst would probably reply (as the late John Maynard Keynes reportedly did): "We shall all be dead by then." To the cynical question What has posterity ever done for me? the generally expectable answer is: "Nothing."[32]

From such responses it is only a short step to the question What do presently living people owe to our cultural past? If the answer is again "Nothing"—or perhaps, "Not much"—one confronts a third, more specific question: Why did so many Americans participate in the celebration of our bicentennial anniversary? If the bicentennial rituals and pageants meant something besides a momentary hubris and perhaps a speculative opportunity to pick up some extra cash, what was its additional significance?

We surmise that most Americans would agree that the bicentennial did have some additional significance but might find it difficult to put this into words. For a good many, we surmise further, the bicentennial was meaningful because it somehow (in different ways for different people) reinforced their identification with an ethos that has helped to carry their nation across the threshold of its third century.

The British ecologist Fraser Darling apparently had something like this in mind when he said: "Tradition and accumulated experience are part of man's environment, and for all the importance of physical and biological factors . . . the ethos is still the biggest ecological factor of all."[33]

Kenneth Boulding (who first asked the question What has posterity ever done for me?) approaches the related question, What do I owe posterity? on the same wavelength, but with an additional twist: "The welfare of the individual depends on the extent to which he can identify himself with others . . . not only with a community in space but also with a community extending over time from the past into the future. . . . a society which loses its identity with posterity and which loses its positive image of the future loses also its capacity to deal with present problems."[34]

An ethos that disclaims any responsibility to posterity exhibits some resemblance to extreme ethnocentrism. An example of the latter is the apparently spreading notion that the United States should aid only those foreign populations in distress that are judged (by American standards) to be salvageable if aided.

We shall return to this so-called lifeboat ethic in chapter 9. Here it is sufficient to ask: If it is deemed ethically defensible to degrade the biosphere to satisfy appetites for luxuries, and if it is likewise deemed defensible to disregard one's own posterity, why, then, is it not just as defensible to give precedence to one's national community if sharing with starving foreigners is judged to endanger one's own amenities?

From this lifeboat ethic applied to foreign populations, it is another short analogical step to a similar attitude toward the poor and destitute within one's own country. That is, if it is deemed morally supportable to deny succor to starving people in other lands, why is it not likewise defensible to ignore poverty wherever it exists?

These centricities evoke questions about still others. Is it ethically defensible to pursue personal gain to the point of weakening the bonds of the community to which one belongs? Is it ethically defensible for individuals to pollute air, water, and land in their quest for personal gain? Or to hoard scarce food, fuel, or other goods, and thereby contribute to the distress of other members of the community? Or to produce large families in a world of dwindling material resources? Or to behave in other ways harmful to individuals, to the nation, to the inchoate world community, or to nonhuman nature, which will likely continue to be one of the determinants of the human future?

We ask these questions and suggest these analogies because

attitudes and principles professed in one context spill over into others. Ethical self-justification by analogy is as pervasive as taxes. Attitudes and norms of interpersonal relations may, and do, influence decisions and practices with regard to degradation of the physical habitat—and vice versa. If the prevailing posture is more exploitive than mutualistic in a society's social environment, it seems likely to be so in its members' relations to the physical habitat too.

⌒⟨ 4 ⟩⌒

Short-Term Benefits
vs. Long-Term Hazards

FORMULATING environmental standards and enacting legislation normally involves a choice between short-term benefits and
longer-term hazards. This unwelcome choice might be called
the time-lag dilemma. It is introduced at this point because it is
closely linked to the conflicting philosophical postures compared in the preceding chapter.

One long-recognized manifestation of this dilemma is the
notorious risk that any short-term benefits achievable by competitive militarism in the nuclear era may be wiped out if prep-
aration of superweapons fails to prevent a thermonuclear holocaust. A more insidious family of risks derives from various
combinations of environmental depletions and pollutions incidental to the pursuit of short-term monetary gains or other
benefits. With few exceptions, the longer-term hazards latent in
such activities are insidious because they take form incremental-
ly. In the main, environmental degradation to date has been a
piecemeal process that gradually grows in magnitude like an
evolving hurricane. Again like cyclonic storms, ecologically disruptive inputs may exhibit positive feedback that produces fresh
inputs until the continuing disaster becomes overwhelming.

The possibility of short-term benefits culminating in destruction of the biosphere is envisioned in numerous contexts. One is
progressive contamination of the oceans by discharge of domes-

tic and industrial refuse. A second is increasing release of waste heat into the atmosphere, a long-term process that may eventually produce radically adverse changes in the earth's regional and global climates. A third is the related possibility that increasing discharge into the atmosphere of various ozone-destructive chemicals may expose the earth's surface to destructive ultraviolet solar radiation. A fourth is the buildup of radioactive pollutions from weapons testing and from a spreading grid of nuclear-fission power reactors. A fifth is the possibility of an unmanageable worldwide imbalance between population growth and food production. A sixth is the emerging technique of genetic engineering, from which some eminent bioscientists fear, at the very least, the accidental release of new pathogens for which no effective therapy is available. Numerous other disruptive possibilities could be cited.

Events may reveal that today's pessimists are too pessimistic, or the optimists too optimistic. However, continuing public debates over short-term benefits versus long-term hazards are alerting more people to possible consequences latent in technological applications of current scientific research. Some of this knowledge will influence those responsible for framing, enacting, and administering policies. Thus, like conflicting philosophical postures, conflicting hypotheses regarding long-term hazards provide significant inputs into the politics of environmental protection.

To explore these hypotheses in detail in all the exigencies in which they may arise would take us far beyond the space available here. Hence, we have chosen to focus the discussion of the time-lag dilemma chiefly on one issue: the hazards of depending increasingly upon electric power generated by nuclear fission to supply the energy demands of the United States and the world as a whole, especially the greater hazards of developing breeder-type fission reactors that extend the accessible reserves of uranium, but at the price of still greater hazards in the long run.

We begin with the concept of ecological demand. This term is verbal shorthand for the rate at which energy and materials are being extracted from nature plus the resultant accumulation of residues that "must go somewhere" at additional cost in energy and materials.

It is difficult—and it may be impossible with available information—to make very reliable calculations regarding the rates and dimensions of total ecological demand in the world as a whole. Nevertheless, the concept directs attention to the trend and interrelatedness of environmental depletions and pollutions, and to the hazards that each of these separately and the two in combination pose for present and future generations.

According to one tentative approximation, global ecological demand increased from 1950 to 1970 about 5 to 6 percent per year. This translates into a doubling period of thirteen to fourteen years.[1] It would be impossible, of course, for any such rate to continue indefinitely. Even a lower rate, and a correspondingly longer doubling period, would contribute another obstacle to infinite economic growth. Such would be true not only in those societies, like the United States, that have attained a high level of income per capita; it would also affect adversely the prospect for major industrialization of many societies in earlier stages of the developmental process. That is, the rate and trend of ecological demand is an important ingredient in the context of environmental politics.

Depletions: Demands and Supplies

Before proceeding with the discussion of the dilemma of short-term boom versus long-term bust, we need a clearer definition of the concept of *resources*. This is a term with many referents. In the broadest sense, a resource is anything that is useful toward achieving a given objective. In political discourse, resources generally refer to money that is spendable by public authorities (hence the expression *disposable resources*).

In other contexts, the referent may be specialized *knowledge*. In this sense, knowledge of atomic structure was just as clearly a resource as the uranium ore mined and refined to produce the first atomic bomb. However, in many contexts, usage restricts resources to physical phenomena: that is, to things extracted directly or indirectly from nature (hence, the expression *natural resources*); more explicitly from land, water, and air, and energy transmitted from the sun. The concept of natural resources is further subdivided into those that are *nonrenewable* and those that are *renewable*. The former denotes things that once used cannot be used again without recycling. Some nonrenewable resources—fossil fuels and other sources of energy—cannot be recycled at all. Others can be, but always with some loss of substance and at some cost in consumption of energy.

Renewable resources are products of biological reproduction: microbes, plants, and animals that contribute to human purposes in various ways. The expression *productive base* of renewable resources refers to factors such as fertile soil, sunlight and water, adequate growing season, a multitude of chemical elements and compounds, and still other requisites. Most if not all of the above concepts are subsumed under the broad concept of *economic* resources: that is, knowledge and materials that enter into the production and distribution of commodities and services.

We have gone into these distinctions here because conflicting notions about resources enter into arguments about the limits of the earth and about potential human ability to overcome or evade them. A widely prevailing view among economists seems to be that physical shortages of accessible energy and most other natural resources, both nonrenewable and renewable, including the productive base of the latter, are unlikely to pose insurmountable obstacles to economic growth throughout any future that they deem relevant to human affairs.

The essence of the contention, as we understand it, is that rising demand for limited available energy and raw materials simply forces up prices. Higher prices, in turn, stimulate research and attract new capital that will make possible drilling deeper oil and gas wells in more inaccessible places, smelting lower-grade ores, inventing substitutes for dwindling natural resources, combating pollutions, and doing whatever else is necessary to sustain the growth process indefinitely. Thus, according to hypothesis, maintaining a balance between rising demands and dwindling natural resources is an economic rather than a physical problem.

Before considering further the supply side of this putative balance, let us look at some prevailing practices and expectations regarding demand—particularly demand for energy, which affects virtually all aspects of supply. As long as fossil fuels and electric power were abundant and relatively cheap, there was little incentive to economize and conserve. Under those halcyon conditions, Americans became not only the world's largest consumers per capita but also the most prodigal wasters.

The physicist Amory Lovins calculates that 250 million Americans consume more energy for air-conditioning alone than more than 800 million Chinese use for everything. In another comparison, he says: "If per capita energy use in the United States were reduced to that of, say, France, the amount 'saved' would suffice to give everyone else in the world nearly a fourth more than he now has." Lovins identifies, in particular, the following areas of gross waste: energy-intensive architecture, mechanized transportation, throwaway containers, short-lived appliances, agricultural practices, and military extravagance.[2]

Others have reached similar conclusions. Numerous analyses seem to be more or less in accord that reducing sheer waste in industry and households could reduce energy consumption 20 to 40 percent or more. Such a saving would go far toward relieving at least temporarily the current energy bind. It would also reduce dependence on unreliable imports, which have actually increased during the seventies. It would buy precious time to work out a rational and less vulnerable energy program.

Thus far, however, reducing direct energy consumption and energy-intensive luxuries seems to be about as popular as a trip to the dentist. At this writing (late 1977), even hesitant steps toward energy conservation have run into stubborn public and legislative resistance. America is still wedded to the mirage of endless economic growth and prodigal, spendthrift energy consumption.

Throughout the 1960s and early 1970s there was a barrage of

optimistic predictions that demand (that is, sales of goods and services) would continue to rise indefinitely by 4 or 6 percent or more annually. Many if not all of these predictions reflected little more than simplistic projections of recent industrial and consumer behavior. Not until the Organization of Petroleum Exporting Countries (OPEC) began shutting off the taps and raising prices could one find much sensible discussion in America, even among professional economists, of the probable availability and price of energy supplies during the rest of this century.[3]

Predictions of perpetually rising consumption have provided propaganda material for those who desire to stimulate demand in order to justify expanding productive capacity. This is a circular forensic gimmick that runs about as follows: People want more automobiles; manufacturers must supply them; automobile drivers want to get there sooner; there must be more superhighways; and so on. A premise of all such thinking, as noted above, is that shortages of materials and energy present no insurmountable obstacles, because supply is defined as an economic, not a physical problem.

A fairly typical exhibit of this reasoning is the critique by economist Carl Kaysen of *The Limits to Growth*, a report circulated in the early seventies.[4] One of the assumptions built into that futuristic model is the physical exhaustibility of nonrenewable resources—energy and materials—in the terrestrial habitat, which, in this respect, is a closed system except for continuing diffuse inputs of solar energy by various processes. Kaysen rejected this assumption, saying in part: "The notion that such limits must exist gains plausibility from the use of physical terms to indicate relevant quantities—[such as] acres of arable land, [or] tons of chrome ore reserves—implicitly invoking the physical finiteness of the earth as the ultimate bound. But this is fundamentally misleading. Resources are properly measured in economic, not physical, terms."[5]

Conventional economic doctrine on this issue is challenged on various grounds. The economist Emile Benoit emphasizes the "esoteric way" that economists define shortages. "So long as prices are free to rise to the level that clears the market [that is, brings supplies and effective demands into balance] there can be no shortages, *by definition*. On this basis, a famine that kills half the population would not be regarded as a food shortage, provided there were no rationing or price controls, and those who could afford it paid the free market price for food." He adds: "I need not underline the peculiarity of this usage."[6]

Critics also question the indefinite accessibility, at *any* price, of energy in concentrated forms required by industrial expansion in more and more countries. Coal, oil, and natural gas are increasingly perceived to be the critical variables, at least for several decades, perhaps much longer. Excluding energy supplied by human and animal muscles, it is estimated that "about 97 percent of primary energy (in the world as a whole) comes from fossil fuels."[7] These fuels cannot be recycled. "Once they are gone they are gone forever." The process is irreversible.[8]

The prospect of continually rising prices and uncertain accessibility of these fuels has stimulated research and experimental development of alternative ways of getting concentrated energy. To date, the most widely and intensively advocated escape from this bottleneck is large-scale development of electric power generated from the heat of nuclear fission.

This course entails severe risks and considerable economic uncertainty. We shall return to the risks later in the chapter. The uncertainty derives from multiplying indications that nuclear fission may not yield much more net energy than the combined energy costs of research, reactors, fuel, operations, security, and permanent safe disposal of worn-out reactors and fuel residues that will remain lethally radioactive for thousands of years.

When and if (still a big IF) it becomes technically possible to derive usable energy from the fusion of light atoms, and if (another big IF) the net energy recovered from that source exceeds substantially the immense costs of research, development, capital, operation, and other functions, then the energy outlook might become less constrictive for a much longer future. In the meantime—a period that may extend for a few decades, or beyond the third century, or perhaps forever—the modes of living to which most peoples in technically advanced societies have become accustomed will continue to depend heavily on the rates of depletion of fossil fuels, supplemented to an uncertain extent by utilization of continuing inputs from the sun.

This conclusion flows directly from the second law of thermodynamics—the principle of entropy. This natural law is not well enough understood by most nonscientists. In lay language, energy from any source cannot be used again as energy in its resultant form. The steam engine provides an example easily understood. Steam is produced by heating water by some energy source, such as fire under the boiler. The heating process transmutes the energy used (say, coal) into inert matter (ashes, in this instance). The steam produced is usable energy that can activate a machine (for example, an electric power generator) or do other work. In the process, the steam loses heat and pressure, and hence its usefulness as an energy source. The steam's energy utility can be restored only by burning more fuel under the boiler; and thus the process of energy depletion continues *in a purely physical manner that has nothing to do with markets and prices*. The same holds for generated electric power. Whether used to produce heat, or light, or motion, or other work, it too loses in the process the capacity for further work.

The main point here is the unidirectional flow of all energy reactions from a state of low entropy to one of higher entropy. In lay language, this means from a state capable of performing work to a state from which no further work can be extracted without restoring the energy source to a state of low entropy: a process that always requires additional expenditure of energy from some other low entropy source—which, in turn, reduces that additional source to high entropy, or uselessness as a source of energy.

Expanding economies, especially industrialized economies, require increasing quantities of concentrated inanimate energy. It seems likely that current levels of production could never have been achieved without abundant, relatively cheap, concentrated energy, predominantly from fossil fuels. It is likewise credible that still unsolved technical problems, especially safe disposal of spent fuels and other residues, along with economic uncertainties that beset large-scale nuclear-fission power development, may yet frustrate the expectations of the scientists, politicians, industrialists, and others who have counted on a major switch to nuclear-fission power.

With processes currently available, concentration of continuing diffuse inputs of solar energy requires expensive consumption of already concentrated energy. For these and some additional reasons, diminishing reserves of easily accessible concentrated energy seem likely to present major obstacles to desired rates of economic growth; and shortages in this sense seem likely to be aggravated by the rapidly increasing numbers of people to be fed for a century or more to come.

From such premises the energy-oriented economist Nicholas Georgescu-Roegen, with growing support from other critics of conventional economic theory, contends that "one of the most enduring myths of the [economic] profession . . . [is] that the price mechanism can offset any shortages, whether of land, energy, or materials," especially energy.[9] The notion of unlimited substitution and invention via scientific research, innovative engineering, and rising prices, he insists, collides head-on with the law of entropy. The most any society can do is to avoid or curtail practices that wastefully continue or accelerate the rate at which accessible concentrated energy is depleted by entropy.

Georgescu and others have suggested that the events of 1973–1974 were a portent of worse in store unless humankind learn to live with the inexorable entropy law. That is, what was perceived by most Americans as a temporary "energy crisis," attributable to governmental bungling and malevolent manipulations by producers and distributors of oil and gas, dramatized the *physical* constraint that diminishing accessibility of abundant, relatively cheap, concentrated energy imposes on continuing progression toward more and more affluence for everyone. The claim that natural resources, especially energy resources, are properly measurable in "economic, not physical terms" holds (if it holds at all) only within the boundaries of *physical* accessibility of *physically* exhaustible resources. Moreover, physical accessibility is subject to the further limiting condition, already noted, that "it takes energy to get energy." The thrust of this proposition is that dwindling reserves of easily accessible energy necessitate going to increasingly complex and costly methods (especially in terms of energy expended) to get less accessible new supplies. In short, what is important is not the *gross* energy underground but the *net* energy recovered.

Many experts have emphasized this point. One of these likens it to the economic law of diminishing returns. Taking the rising cost of recovering fossil petroleum, he says: "From 1860 to 1870, the average depth at which oil was found was 300 feet. By 1900, the average find was at 1,000 feet. By 1927, it was 3,000 feet; [in 1974] . . . 6,000 feet. Drilling deeper and deeper into the earth to find scattered oil deposits requires more and more energy." The same and other experts find the net return from producing oil from Rocky Mountain shale comparably unpromising from an economic standpoint.[10] The same kind of problem confronts *every* proposal to develop new sources of energy, whether from nuclear fission, nuclear fusion, geothermal reservoirs, wind-driven generators, solar-heat receptors, or other sources.

After reviewing what is known about the energy and other costs of getting energy from new sources, the economist Anne Carter emphasized, in 1974, the complexity and uncertainties in all calculations to date. Her tentative conclusion was that, if one accepts the assumption of continued 3 percent annual increase in energy demand, "the combined effects of increasing energy consumption coefficients and the more costly new energy technologies would place a strong drag on the economy."[11] Reading between the lines, we surmise that she is warning her fellow Americans that much more will have to be done about reducing consumption before the energy problem can be brought under control.

Shifting from economic costs to technical feasibilities, one finds numerous physical scientists expressing confidence that pure and applied science can cope with depletions of energy and materials. The geochemist Harrison Brown is a fair representative of this optimism. As early as 1954, he anticipated increasingly large inputs of scientific knowledge to compensate for progressive depletions of high-grade, easily accessible energy and materials extracted from nature.

Two years later he added: "As time goes by and . . . deposits of high-grade ores are exhausted, we will approach asymptotically the condition wherein machine civilization is fed entirely by the processing of lowest common denominators—air, sea water, ordinary rock, and sunlight." [12]

More recently, Brown has added an important caveat, saying: *"From a purely technological point of view,* man could in principle live comfortably on a combination of his own trash and the leanest of earth substances." [13] The thrust of this caveat is that an increasingly complex machine civilization, dependent upon the above materials, is credible only on the assumption that those who rule can prevent serious accidents, illicit interventions, and technical failures, both domestically and internationally, continuously for thousands of years into an unknown future.

No such stability and continuity have ever been even remotely approached anywhere upon the earth. It seems to us extremely unlikely that they can be attained within any relevant future in our politically fragmented world, characterized by extremes of wealth and destitution within and among countries, by conflicting images of what is desirable and possible, and by frustrations, hostilities, and recurrent outbreaks of violence within and between nations.

Still more recently, Brown told the officers of the Rockefeller Foundation: "If I were to place a bet on the next hundred years, I would say that the rich countries are destined to disappear and the earth as a whole to revert to systems more like those of the poor countries. . . . The problems that stand in our way" are not scientific and technological, but "are mainly social and political." [14]

Read in context, these and further statements by Brown and others seem to envisage the demise of current-style industrial civilization as a consequence of the big bang of thermonuclear war. Without depreciating that hazard in the slightest, we envision a less abrupt but no less destructive outcome of present trends: namely a gradual rundown of the biotic clock.

How long might it take for such a rundown to reach a point of no return? Some anticipate hundreds of years; others, a century or less if current rates of denudation and disruption are allowed to continue. No one really knows. However, there seems to be close to consensus that abundant accessible energy in concentrated packages is a sine qua non for the survival of technically and economically complex societies, the United States above all.

The disagreement arises in part from different time-scales of conjecture, in part from varying degrees of faith regarding future breakthroughs in pure and applied science, and in part, also, from assumptions (usually tacit) regarding the stability and continuity of political institutions and the social order to which these are responsive.

In our view, it is sheer fantasy to assume a political/social order sufficiently continuous and stable to sustain a high-income machine civilization running on the low-grade materials that would be accessible in a denuded and disrupted habitat. But this question plainly needs more research and reflection.

Hazards: Present and Future

Suppose that scientific research and innovative engineering can reduce or eradicate most of the conditions that seriously pollute air, water, and land; that contaminate food; that produce noise physiologically injurious as well as aesthetically disturbing; that render farms, mines, factories, trains, planes, highways, and other working places needlessly unsafe not only for the workers but also for everyone else in the vicinity. There still remains the question whether the political system, and the social forces to which it is responsive, will tolerate effective remedies before it is too late to matter.

This question deserves more attention for several reasons. One is the issue of economic impact. Whatever remedy is contemplated, as Boulding (among others) contends, "the problem is complicated by the fact that almost anything we do about the environment is likely to have considerable effect on the distribution of income and wealth." [15] If this is so, and we can think of no credible ground for doubting it, then the critical issue becomes: How much is likely to be undertaken when effective action of any kind seems almost certain to affect more or less adversely the employment, profits, conveniences, and luxuries of those elements of the community to whom public authorities are significantly responsive? In no type of case, so far as we are aware, has the choice between acting effectively now, or passing as much of the risk as possible to future generations, surfaced more starkly than in the acrimonious disputations over large-scale nuclear-fission power.

The public domain has been flooded with warnings from physicists, ecologists, a few economists, and various other concerned citizens. These warnings apply not only to the hazards entailed for presently living people, but also to the ethics of creating monstrous hazards through a future many times longer than any civilization has survived in the past. Warnings deal with risks of accidents, technical malfunction, thefts of plutonium and other radioactive materials, and unsolved (perhaps unsolvable) problems of where and how to dispose safely of worn-out reactors, spent fuel, and other residues that emit lethal radiation virtually forever.

It seems likely that these and other hazards can be reduced somewhat—at a price not always mentioned by advocates of nuclear-fission power. However, our response again is that *reasonable safety from such monstrous risks assumes a stability and continuity of the political/social order never attained in the past, and even less credibly expectable in the present era of radical change, unrest, and violence.*

Physicist Alvin Weinberg, outspoken advocate of prompt, large-scale development of a nuclear-fission power industry, understands these hazards. In a widely quoted article in *Science* a few years ago, he said: "We nuclear people have made a Faustian bargain with society. On the one hand, we offer . . . an inexhaustible source of energy . . . cheaper than energy from fossil fuel . . . when properly handled . . . almost nonpolluting. . . . But the price we demand of society for this magical source is both a vigilance and a longevity of our social institutions that we are quite unaccustomed to."[16]

One can admire Weinberg's candor but still entertain serious doubt as to his longer-range prescience. For reasons he himself acknowledges, his "Faustian bargain" is a poor one at best. In the light of all human experience, it offers extremely dangerous goods at a price that includes monstrous hazards virtually forever. As Professor Richard Falk starkly puts it: "Merely stating the issue exposes its folly."[17]

More recently Weinberg has tried to counter the argument of social-political hazard by invoking the high standard of risk-assessment and prudence that, he says, prevails in scientific laboratories.[18] We do not question the strength or sincerity of his conviction. However, in the half-century that we have lived and worked in university environments, there have been many unanticipated accidents in carefully organized, administered, and supervised laboratories. In recent years there have also been accidents with vehicles and planes carrying nuclear materials. We simply cannot imagine a milieu in which human failures and technical malfunctions never occur. Moreover, even if such a milieu could be created, Weinberg's suggestion that political institutions and operations can be made even as reliable as scientific laboratories seems to us dangerously unrealistic. It ignores the adversary confrontation that is the very essence of every political system, along with the conflicting forces and pressures to which politicians are continuously subjected. Hence, the analogy seems to us irrelevant as well as seductively misleading and dangerous, especially so in an era as unsettled and recurrently violent as ours promises to be indefinitely. The human record offers no assurance whatever that even a repressive regime run by scientists and technologists could eradicate, or for that matter significantly reduce, the hazards of a technology so demanding as nuclear-fission power.

There is also an important ethical issue: "Several billion people are being asked to sign by proxy an irrevocable Faustian bargain whose small print they have not read and are told they cannot understand, and those perhaps most affected—thousands of generations yet unborn—are not consulted at all." [19]

A notable feature of the disputations over Weinberg's Faustian bargain is the reiteration that the hazard is no greater, probably less, than many others humankind have learned to live with. Sometimes the comparison is between conditions in technically advanced contemporary societies and those in preindustrial societies past and present. In other cases stress is laid upon the risks which people even in our own society simply take for granted, such as death by automobile accident, or illness from polluted air or water, or the risks "from food additives and drugs, from earthquakes, from the failure of dams, from the shipment and storage of chemicals, from the burning of coal," and much else. Statistics are presented to support the claim that the odds of serious disasters from nuclear-fission operations are minute compared with ordinary hazards to which people everywhere are exposed. [20]

Attempts to justify a nuclear-fission-based economy by such comparisons may be seductive but are also misleading. In no previous era have human activities created hazards that can endanger human existence virtually forever. Comparison of the duration of hazard is simply omitted from most of the propaganda for a large-scale shift to a nuclear-fission economy—or as Schumacher might put it, here is a prescription to resolve a short-term predicament by creating a far more dangerous long-term hazard. [21]

Three additional interrelated issues have lurked backstage throughout the preceding discussion of the dilemma of short-term gains versus long-term (as well as short-term) hazards. These ancillary issues deserve specific attention before we bring this chapter to a close.

Time, Irreversibility, and Burden of Proof

The lapse of time between causative condition and reasonably conclusive attribution of damage therefrom is not a new phenomenon. Humankind have always had to live with delayed consequences of past events. Past-minded optimists reiterate that delayed effects have rarely been irreparable—so why let conjectured future hazards cripple the onward march toward bigger and allegedly better achievements?

Such optimism disregards a relatively new dimension of vulnerability. Introduction of nuclear weapons presented the unprecedented possibility of a man-made catastrophe that might abruptly push humankind over the precipice. Cumulative denudation, pollution, and disruption of the biosphere pose a comparable hazard, though probably through a longer, more complicated, and much more *insidious* process. We emphasize insidious because environmental degradation is a resultant of countless interrelated events, small events in the main, often disregarded at the time of occurrence, but building piece by piece into a cumulative threat that at long last is evoking serious questions as to its impact on the human prospect.

The insidious nature of this piecemeal disruption of the life-sustaining biosphere presents problems with which neither politicians nor most of their constituents are well equipped to cope. Environmental politics, like all politics, is geared to short-term problems and solutions, often to procrastination. However, we have reached a point where sweeping long-term environmental hazards under the carpet is no longer safe, even if viewed as smart politics. The consequence of neglect and procrastination is exemplified by the prolonged failure to prepare for the energy shortage, long anticipated and publicly predicted by qualified experts. It was, and still is, politically safer to permit, even to encourage, wasteful consumption of fuel and power—and hope that something will turn up to make restrictive action unnecessary—than to impose unpopular conservation measures before the predicted bind is actually much more widely experienced.

Longer-range planning is also handicapped by limited knowledge and by disagreements among presumably qualified experts. Consider, for example, the inconclusive debates over the possible consequences of discharging ever-increasing quantities of CO_2 into the atmosphere from burning fossil fuels. Will this produce another ice age, as some scientists have predicted? Or will it melt the polar ice and inundate most of the world's major cities, as others, comparably qualified, anticipate? Or will there be no significant impact at all on the human future?

In this as in many other cases involving futuristic uncertainty, it seems likely that most public authorities will prefer to wait and see; that there will be public opposition to restrictions that will hurt or inconvenience many; and that most people will ignore the whole business and go about their affairs as usual.

These generalizations may be too pessimistic. It has proved possible to mobilize public and government when the disputed hazard was an increase of birth defects or incurable diseases. This was evident in the notorious thalidomide episode, and likewise in the public response to the threat of cancer from strontium 90 fallout from nuclear weapons testing in the atmosphere. Something similar seems to underlie a fairly widespread anxiety regarding risks from promiscuous use of long-persisting pesticides, from dumping lethal chemicals into public waterways, and from many other environmental hazards.

However, venerable common-law doctrines present obstacles to timely protection against predicted hazards as well as to actual damage. One is that a complainant must show actual damage or risk of damage in order to acquire "standing to sue." Another is the authority of a court to disallow a "class action." A third, perhaps most important, is the doctrine that the "burden of proof rests on the complainant."[22]

Because litigation is expensive, and because private individuals damaged or exposed to damage so often lack the necessary dollars to defend their rights in court, they usually cannot afford to sue even if they could make an excellent prima facie case. The logical recourse in many environmental causes is for a group of individuals with similar claims to band together in a "class action." However, American judges have generally denied "standing to sue" in such cases, though a few judges have taken a strong stand against this ancient obstacle to justice.[23]

More apparent progress is being made in attacks from various sources on the historic rule that the "burden of proof" rests on the party seeking a remedy. This doctrine has been repeatedly invoked to legitimize inaction or denial of preventive action in environmental cases, despite near certainty that no conclusive proof can be established until irreparable damage has actually occurred. This legal relic of a bygone age has been asserted in legislative hearings, in public propaganda, as well as in the courts, in attempts to block protective action until dead bodies are produced, so to speak.

Modification of the ancient doctrine that burden of proof rests upon the complainant is gradually gaining ground. There is a slowly expanding corpus of environmental law—legislation, administration, and court decisions—in which public authority sets standards, and gives litigants a right to protection in anticipation of future damage, that is, before actual damage can be proved conclusively to have occurred.

This change puts the producers of new drugs, food additives, pesticides, or other commodities under obligation to prove no significant risk of future damage, instead of requiring the defendant to prove that the product in dispute has caused actual damage. The same modification is emerging in suits over the hazards of working places such as mines, factories, and so on. In short, the shift enables judges in an expanding variety of cases to award injunctions or other protection against reasonably established hazards before rather than merely after actual damage has been incurred.

Business managements and business-related organizations have strongly resisted relaxing the historic rule. A typical exhibit is a published statement by a spokesman for the National Association of Manufacturers (NAM). "The petitioner who alleges a health hazard should have to prove affirmatively that such a health hazard exists; it should not be the defendant's burden to prove that none exists. The difficulties that arise from having to prove a 'negative' are overwhelming, and inasmuch as the courts have justly placed the burden of proof in the past on the party alleging harm, the doctrine should not be abandoned now."[24]

In an exchange between the NAM and Harvard biologist John T. Edsall, chairman of the Committee on Scientific Freedom and Responsibility of the American Association for the Advancement of Science, the latter declared emphatically that "new reagents introduced into industry on a large scale should be regarded as dangerous until proved safe."[25]

Similar demands for reversing the traditional "proof" doctrine have arisen in many recent contexts: nuclear-power development, recombinant DNA research, supersonic aviation, food additives, new medical therapies, and others. In nearly every instance, demands for reversal emphasize the time-lag between exposure and causal connection with damages.

In many instances it may be difficult to prove conclusively either a positive or a negative case with regard to hazards. But this difficulty does not dispose of the ethical issue implicit in the burden-of-proof controversy. How much risk *should* be tolerated in the face of reasonable doubt as to the long-term consequences—of genetic engineering, for example. This is a political, not a scientific, question. And a strong case can be made that it should be answered by public authorities, in the light of ethical as well as pragmatic considerations.

The issues of "standing to sue," "class actions," and "burden of proof" are by no means settled at this writing. But they keep surfacing in one context after another. Industry's spokesmen and many scientists will probably continue to resist reversal of the traditional doctrines. It seems just as likely that these legal obstructions to effective environmental protection will find their way to the slowly expanding graveyard of obsolete law.

Latent in much of the controversy over shifting the burden of proof from complainant to defendant is the question of irreversibility. This issue arises in at least four contexts. It can refer to death of an individual or extinction of a species; to progression of a disease for which no cure is available; to trends in the physical environment that it may become impossible at some point to arrest with any available technology; and to trends in the social milieu that are irreversible only in the sense that the community in question cannot, or will not, pay the cost of arresting a dysfunctional trend that it is technically possible to reverse.

The first two kinds need no elaboration. The third is exemplified in the controversy regarding the life-supportive prospects of the biosphere. When ecologists and others express concern lest continuation of current trends render the earth progressively less fit for human habitation, they are envisioning irreversibility in a sense analogous to the death of an individual or extinction of a species.

The fourth kind of irreversibility—in which conditions and trends not inherently irreversible in any absolute sense—may become so in a practical sense, because of resistance to the capital cost and social changes that would be required to arrest the trend in question. This fourth kind of irreversibility, which might be called social irreversibility, is exemplified in the public resistance that would certainly block any legislation to outlaw private ownership of motor vehicles; or, a different kind of resistance, to restoring to food production the millions of fertile American acres annually transmuted into hard-surface highways and grandiose shopping centers.

All four kinds of situation add up to a strong case for shifting the burden of proof to those who would introduce potentially dysfunctional innovations, including projects literally "set in concrete" or other refractory materials that degrade the physical habitat.[26]

Before extending the horizon of the landscape of environmental politics, we pause to review the terrain reconnoitered thus far. We have compared certain ways of thinking about and reacting to the progressive degradation of our terrestrial habitat.

We have noted in chapter 1 the terrestrial impact of extraterrestrial phenomena, and the destructive phenomena of terrestrial nature. We have emphasized, in particular, human activities that, either by themselves or in combination with nonhuman phenomena, have acceleratively depleted, polluted, and disrupted the habitat from which humankind derive subsistence.

Unprecedented population growth and concomitant enlargement of exploitive capabilities continue to degrade this habitat. We have noted some indications of awakening awareness of hazards implicit in progressive environmental degradation. However, there is a pervasive countertendency, within the United States and in other high-income societies, to view such deterioration with equanimity, as a source of mild discomfort and inconvenience but scarcely a threat to the human future.

Conventional economic theory as well as nearly universal faith in applied science and innovative technology contribute to this image. Despite challenges from diverse sources, some such expectation continues to buttress confidence in ability to carry on indefinitely to ever-higher levels of material abundance.

The credibility of this expectation is brought into question in numerous contexts. One of these with which we shall be centrally concerned in the remaining chapters is the proliferation of vulnerabilities that accompanies progression to higher levels of technology and economic versatility and complexity. We are now ready to extend the horizon to encompass more of these competing vulnerabilities that affect what is undertaken to protect individuals and communities from damage and hazards deriving from changes in the physical habitat.

~(5)~

Domestic Social Context

MOST AMERICANS possess or have access to amenities as well as elemental necessities beyond anything attainable anywhere in the not-so-distant past. All but the very poor and destitute enjoy a material standard of living beyond the reach of any but a tiny elite in scores of countries in earlier stages of economic modernization today.

However, all material things carry a price tag; or as ecologists and economists remind us, there is "no free lunch." Part of the price of progression to higher levels of material affluence has been progressive deterioration of the physical fundament upon which the national community is built. Some in our midst perceive this deterioration to be an obstacle not only to still greater abundance but even to maintenance for much longer of levels already achieved. Part of this concern arises from the extent and rate of environmental depletions, pollutions, and disruptions. Concern derives also from the many other vulnerabilities that have coincided with increasingly complex organizations and relationships, and from the steeply rising cost of combating vulnerabilities from all sources. The function of this chapter is to identify and assess some of the societal vulnerabilities that affect what is undertaken with regard to damage and hazards that derive from a deteriorating physical habitat.

Disruption of Essential Services

Industrialized urban societies depend upon reliable delivery of a long list of essential goods and services. Conversely, they are critically vulnerable to actual or threatened interruptions. Disruption may result from at least three kinds of events: deliberate withholding or withdrawal by those who produce and deliver goods and perform other essential services; illicit interventions that disrupt production, delivery, or other performance; and accidents caused by human failures or technical malfunctions.

Deliberate Withholding and Withdrawal. Actual or threatened disruptions come from both ends of the economic spectrum: from those who plan and manage production and distribution, and from those who carry out their directives.

All economies are subject to withholdings and withdrawals at the management end. Centrally planned and administered systems under authoritarian management give and withhold to suit the purposes of their rulers who can generally, at least temporarily, disregard the elemental needs and desires of their citizens. In market-type economies, business managements may operate nearly as arbitrarily. Mergers and other operations in restraint of trade are endemic. Managements may put new patents "into the refrigerator." They can, and sometimes do, depress quality to shorten the life of goods produced; shut down plants or threaten to; suspend transportation; deny credit; and employ various other tactics to enlarge profits by coercing labor, government, or the community as a whole.

Rarely does a month pass without public disclosure of disruptive actions or threats by managements. One even finds business pitted against government itself: for example, the oblique threat to blackmail New Jersey in reprisal against efforts by the governor and legislature to free funds of the New York/ New Jersey Port Authority, desperately needed to subsidize mass transportation in the metropolitan area. It was asserted publicly that "if New Jersey can act so cavalierly with respect to one group of bondholders, then all of us in the financial community must make a careful reevaluation of all the state's outstanding debt obligations and its future financings."[1]

Most Americans in positions to influence public policy have been traditionally tolerant of such behavior by corporate managements. But that does not make the behavior any less serious a threat to individuals, local communities, and even to the nation as a whole. At the very least, *it increases the cost of essential goods and services, and thereby indirectly affects the allocation of disposable resources for all purposes.*

Those who work at the grass roots—or upon the scaffoldings and asphalt, so to speak—have also learned to withhold and withdraw their services, or to threaten to do so, as a means of attaining desired objectives. We refer, of course, to organized absenteeism, slowdowns, refusal to cross picket lines, and other disruptive actions by those who harvest crops, work in mines and factories, operate commercial vehicles and planes, process and deliver food supplies, collect garbage and trash, attend to water supplies and sewage disposal, tend power and transportation grids, control takeoffs and landings in airports, deliver mail and freight, staff schools and universities, fight fires, maintain civic order, and perform many other services essential, in some instances vital, to the continued functioning of a complex modern society.

It is almost a truism that *the higher the level of technological-economic development, and the more dense and urbanized the society, the more dependent its members become on the uninterrupted delivery of essential services.*

In retrospect, it seems remarkable that this elemental reality should have gone so long virtually unnoticed. There is a hint of this source of fragility in a few pre-1970 writings.[2] More recently there has been spreading recognition in news reporting, editorializing, and other writing.

The economist Robert Heilbroner, for example, noted (in 1971) the recent discovery of the extreme vulnerability of service-dependent societies to labor stoppages. "In 'old-fashioned' capitalism one could buffer the effects of a strike by living off inventories of coal and steel while labor and management fought it out. But there are no inventories of garbagemen's or teachers' or flight controllers' services. An urbanized economy is critically dependent upon the regular performance of its service tasks."[3]

What this urban fragility may portend has been fleetingly revealed on numerous occasions: by strikes of trash and garbage collectors, truck drivers, air controllers, postmen, firefighters, schoolteachers, and many other performers of essential services. The extent of urban vulnerability has been starkly revealed by partial and total walkouts of the police in a few cities. It was also driven home by the specter of a spreading epidemic toward the end of the prolonged garbage collectors' strike in New York City in 1968.[4] In 1974 a strike of municipal employees in San Francisco came close to shutting down that city for nine days. One especially serious consequence of this paralysis was the spillage of "some 100 million gallons of raw sewage . . . into the bay every day." It is likewise significant in this, as in similar mass withdrawals of essential services, that the strikers won most of their demands previously rejected by the city government.[5]

It was long taken for granted by politicians and other elites that those who perform vital civic services would continue to do so; if necessary, they would be compelled to. Or alternatively, it was assumed that the government could always call on the military to take over in an emergency. For political as well as technical reasons, the credibility of these assumptions is being challenged today in many places and situations.

Newspaper editors and others who purport to speak for the public interest declaim that strikes in essential services are intolerable—as indeed they are. Legislatures have enacted laws forbidding strikes against the government and imposing severe penalties on individual strikers, union officials, and union treasuries. Editorials and letters to the editor belabor judges for failing to enforce such laws more rigorously. Anguished victims demand protection from the pressure—often characterized by the ugly word *blackmail*—exerted by those who normally perform the disrupted or threatened services. Some recommend calling on the National Guard or even the regular army to take over disrupted services and break strikes, regardless of the risk that lurks in pitting soldiers against civilians in a democratic society.

Despite all counterefforts, disruptions of essential services continue to recur. It is reported that the number of public-employee strikes at all levels of government in the United States rose from 36 in 1960 to 412 in 1970. This increase occurred, moreover, in the face of laws forbidding such strikes against the federal government and thirty-three of the state governments. As one investigator wryly observes, "usually such laws have about as much effectiveness as a paper fence."[6]

Preoccupation with strikes against government should not be allowed to divert attention from the community's vulnerability to lockouts, strikes, and other disruptions in private industries, especially those providing vital public services such as fuel and power, transport and communications, and some others. It is also noteworthy that the disruptive impact on the community can be grossly out of proportion to the number of strikers. An example, in 1974, was the ability of a tiny branch of the United Mine Workers—responsible for maintaining structures in coal mines—to keep a large part of the country's mines closed "because of a firm tradition that no miner will cross a picket line, even if the line consists of a single worker."[7]

A further risk lurks in the opportunities that disruptions of services afford to individuals prone to violence. This traditional vulnerability was exhibited in the destruction of printing equipment by some of the pressmen engaged in the strike against the *Washington Post* in 1975. One conclusion that emerges from that kind of vandalism is that the more technically complex the mechanisms and processes through which an essential service is delivered, the greater becomes the opportunity of striking workers not only to withdraw their personal services but also to prevent others from taking over.

As previously emphasized, the leverage which both managements and unions are able to exert on the community derives to a large extent from the critical dependence of dense and complex communities on continuity of services. Criminal or other sanctions may punish individuals, but experience to date seems to indicate that such methods may not restore the disrupted service, and may even spread the damage by provoking sympathy strikes in other industries.

At the very least, these dependencies increase the cost of services, either directly in higher prices or indirectly in higher taxes. In either case, one consequence is some reallocation of resources. This may or may not degrade the quality of the physical environment. We say "may or may not" because strikes and threats of strikes increasingly include demands for safer and more healthful working places—such as, say, cleaner air in mines and factories. The cost, whether in prices or in taxes, must be borne by someone.

Illicit Interventions. Essential services are also vulnerable to interventions by blackmailers, saboteurs, hijackers, revolutionary terrorists, pathological criminals, and other illicit interveners. This kind of disruption is not a new phenomenon. But making it increasingly ominous are the expanding opportunities for disruption afforded by the combination of new destructive tools and the technological complexity, economic interdependence, and human density of industrial-urban communities.

Illicit interventions have become front-page news. One could cite hundreds of recent statements addressed to the damage and risks attributed thereto. A few will suffice, but first, a concise overview from a physical scientist: "More and more, human life is being welded into a vast interdependent network. . . . We rely on an increasingly complicated system of waterlines, power tools, relays, pumps, boilers, switches and generators. . . . The fragile, overstrained chains of supplying communications, energy, water and food can be cut at any link. As more links are forged, more options are opened for disruption."[8]

It has been repeatedly asserted, by persons who should know whereof they speak, that under present and prospective conditions a mere platoon of sophisticated saboteurs could paralyze

New York or any other large city in several different ways—among others, by poisoning the water supply or disrupting the flow of electric power. Summarizing expert testimony on the latter in an article entitled "The Fragile Cities," James Reston reported in 1971 that "fifty key electrical workers, going down the right manholes, could paralyze every electrical circuit . . . in Manhattan."[9]

Douglas DeNike, a clinical psychologist, stresses additional dimensions of risk: malevolent criminality and mental illness. Given the number of persons so afflicted and at large, the threat of illicit intervention takes another leap upward.[10]

Mobility adds still another dimension. An analysis focused primarily, though not exclusively, on skyjacking sums up this opportunity for illicit intervention: "The detection of the bandits becomes increasingly difficult in the impersonal society of mass transport. . . . The outlaws' ability to disrupt air traffic—or any other modern standardized process—is increasing proportionally with the functional complexity of the process itself, and parallel to the destructive power at their disposal."[11]

For several very cogent reasons, discussion of illicit intervention has come to a focus on nuclear power-development and weapons plants, especially the so-called breeder reactors with their production of plutonium. Ralph Lapp was one of the pioneers, among nuclear scientists, to spell out the enormity of this hazard. He called it the "ultimate threat," and envisioned blackmail of whole nations by means of illicitly acquired mini-bombs armed with plutonium.

His thesis and argument ran about as follows: The quantity of plutonium that destroyed Nagasaki in 1945 was no larger than a baseball. The development of breeder reactor plants is already giving more and more persons in private industry as well as in government laboratories and factories easy access to plutonium stocks. Increasing accessibility multiplies the difficulties (to which one could add *costs*) of preventing theft of this super-explosive. Existing methods of transporting plutonium offer multiple opportunities for hijacking and other modes of theft. It is now technically possible to design plutonium minibombs small enough to fit into an ordinary travel case. There have already been incidents (each of which fortunately proved to be a hoax) that indicate beyond question the feasibility of holding a city or even an entire nation hostage.[12]

With the exportation of nuclear-fission equipment and technology to countries whose leaders are bent on wresting wealth and power from the older industrial societies, blackmail becomes an ever more sinister ingredient of the context of environmental politics at both domestic and international levels, about which, more in the next chapter.

Whether adequate defenses can be devised against nuclear theft—especially in transit—remains to be demonstrated. That effective protection against theft and illicit use of stolen material, even if technically possible, *will add another expensive item to the cost of energy, and of societal protection, seems as certain as taxes.*

Judging from reliable sources, the record to date is one of lax standards and slack security. Theodore B. Taylor, a nuclear physicist and a recognized authority in this domain, has publicly stated: "We guard our money much better than we have guarded, are guarding, or will guard our nuclear material. . . . The overwhelming majority of plant managers I talked to said they couldn't stop theft by a large group of professionals. We need more guards, fences, alarms and surveillance."[13] *All* these are additional sources of higher costs.

Since plutonium emits lethal radiation through 200,000 years, with a half-life of 25,000 years, the hazard from illicit interventions involving this material is not merely monstrous blackmail and terrorism, but an ever-present danger that, through malevolence as well as accident, large cities, larger regions, even entire countries might be rendered uninhabitable for periods extending into the future thousands of years longer than the building of the pyramids is distant from the present.

Put in the form of a more general hypothesis: The higher the level of destructive instruments accessible to saboteurs, terrorists, pathological criminals, or other illicit interveners, and the more mobile and complex national societies and the inchoate world community become, the larger become the opportunities for illicit interventions that entail hazards comparable to those of a war fought with thermonuclear missiles—and the higher climbs the cost of providing even minimal protection against such illicit interveners.

Disruptive Accidents. A third cluster of service disruptions derives from accidental breakdowns, previously considered (in chapter 4) in the context of the dilemma of short-term gains and long-term hazards. Accidental breakdowns may result from destructive phenomena of nature, from human failure, or from technical malfunctions. The strong odds of their occurrence is expressed in the often-quoted maxim, "If anything can go wrong it will."

The hazards of accidents have long been recognized in mining, farming, lumbering, manufacturing, transportation, power transmission, and many other operations. What is relatively new is the rapidly expanding magnitude of disruption that accidents can produce, and the concomitantly rising cost of providing backup facilities or other safeguards against the disruptive, even paralyzing, effects of accidental breakdowns.

These trends add further dimensions to the dilemma of short-term gains versus long-term hazards. The issue has come sharply into focus in the continuing debate over increasing reliance on electricity generated by nuclear fission. It is likewise central to the emerging biochemical agenda of DNA research and development of genetic engineering.

In the case of nuclear power, hazards arise not only from illicit interventions, but also from the proneness of reactors to malfunction and from the difficulty of preventing accidental leakage of their radioactive fuels and residues into the human environment. With the widely advocated shift toward "breeder-type" reactors, fueled with plutonium, these hazards are vastly magnified. Hazards of comparable disruptive potential are claimed by many eminent scientists to be latent in the possibility that accident may permit man-made organisms of extreme virulence to escape from biochemical laboratories.

While specialists dispute the likelihood of serious accidents and the extent and severity of damage if accidents do occur, as all human experience assures that they will, nonexpert citizens are left without adequate guidance even as to the issues at stake. Plainly there is insufficient space here to review the massive volume of evidence, conjecture, and especially, self-serving propaganda that enshrouds these issues. The most we can do is to indicate some of the hazards and cite a few assessments that seem to us to be competent and prudent.

Critics of nuclear-power development contend that the risks of accidents both in operations and in disposal of lethal residues are too great and potential damage too terrible and lasting to be tolerated. For a lucid, nontechnical, and fair assessment, we go to the economist Allen Kneese.

His main thesis is that large-scale nuclear-fission power development "will impose a burden of continuous monitoring and sophisticated management of a dangerous material, essentially forever. The penalty of not bearing this burden may be unparalleled disaster. This irreversible burden would be imposed even if nuclear fission were to be used only for a few decades."

It is impossible here to review at length the hazards that Kneese identifies with a large-scale plutonium power industry, hazards that would menace future generations as well as presently living people. He describes the extreme toxicity of plutonium and the multiplicity of ways in which it could escape into the environment. In addition to human error and technical malfunctions, he concludes: "When one factors in the possibility of sabotage and warfare, where power plants are prima facie targets not just in the United States but also in less developed countries, then there is almost no limit to the size of the catastrophe one can envisage." [14]

Accidental leakage from stored residues present comparable risks, for which no reliable solution is known at present. Taking one example, the fifty million gallons of radioactive residues already accumulated in temporary storage by 1973 in tanks near the nuclear weapons plant at Hanford, Washington, the chemist J. C. Giddings says: "The tanks require constant cooling and maintenance; if a temporary halt should occur in the routine of

civilization in the next few centuries, spillage could be catastrophic." Later in the same assessment he cites still another
source of hazard: unpredictable accidents not directly originating within the nuclear power complex. He notes that a B-52
bomber crashed only five miles from a nuclear power plant in
Michigan, and then concludes: "If there is a slipup or a miscal-
culation or a peculiar geological event [for example, an earthquake near a storage site] in the next few hundred years, mankind could suffer enormously." [15]

It is widely assumed that no hazard is so great that resulting
damage will be irreparable. This assumption is repeatedly asserted regarding the risks implicit in a nuclear-fission power
industry. To this assumption the nuclear physicist John Gofman
makes the obvious rejoinder: "The only way nuclear power
would ever be conceivably safe would be if you had a society of
perfect human beings totally robotized, where no materials ever
failed, no directions were ever followed poorly, where no sabotage ever existed, where no acts of God ever occurred, where
there were no psychotics, no angry people, a society that no one
has ever remotely visualized. . . . The absurdity of a society of
that sort is so self-evident that we long ago should have stopped
the nonsense of nuclear fission energy." [16]

In the widening debate evoked by the trauma of empty gasoline pumps, colder buildings, lower speed limits, and steeply
rising prices for all forms of energy and nearly everything else,
several attitudes have become more clearly evident. Many advocates of getting on quickly with nuclear-fission power development exhibit gross ignorance of the enduring hazards entailed.
Others, including plenty of scientists and engineers as well as
economists and even some professional students of government, recognize the risks but assume a perfection of safeguards
and a degree and continuity of public order never remotely approached in any era. Still others reveal themselves to be simply
short-term maximizers who put profits, kudos, comforts, or
convenience above responsibility for bequeathing so monstrous
a hazard and burden to their descendants. The further one
probes into these matters, the clearer it becomes how few people

recognize responsibility for, or even give much thought to, a future that extends very far beyond their own brief tenure of life.

Be that as it may, we perceive no credible escape from the conclusion that part of the trade-off for short-term benefits from increasingly complex technology and economy is a corresponding increase of vulnerability to accidents as well as to illicit interventions and other disruptions of the services upon which contemporary complex urban societies inexorably depend for survival. Some disruptions directly affect the physical habitat adversely. In addition, the larger and more complex the economy, and the technology that supports it, the greater becomes the necessity to divert resources from other purposes to provide even minimal protection. And if standby facilities are provided to take over in case of breakdowns, the diversion of resources becomes still higher.[17]

Community Erosion

Disruptions of essential services may be symptoms of a still more debilitating trend: insidious erosion of the political community. By community erosion we mean piecemeal crumbling of the social cement—a metaphor for the linkages of identification, loyalty, civic confidence, and so forth, that distinguish a functioning political-social order from a condition of dissolution and anarchy. The hypothesis here is that a national community is currently and prospectively viable—that is, capable of functioning and presumably durable—only so long as most of its members identify with it, accept the legitimacy of its public authorities, conform in the main to its legal and other norms, and derive a sense of support and security from identifying with the community.

Vulnerability surfaces if and as these linkages are broken or exhibit excessive strain. Symptoms of erosion may include such things as escalating discontent with the existing distribution of wealth, income, and opportunity; venomous interclass, ethnic, or racial animosities; loss of confidence in public authorities and other civic leaders; spreading vandalism, arson, theft, and personal molestation; growing anonymity and anomie; and much else in addition. Community erosion is plainly occurring if increasing numbers silently withdraw from identification and participation in community rituals and other civic activities, or if they limp along in fatalistic frustrated apathy, or strive overtly or covertly to destroy the existing social-political order.[18]

An advanced stage of community erosion may portend early dissolution of the political system and its supportive social order. Nothing so extreme is suggested here with reference to the United States. But disquieting symptoms of community erosion are evident to many observers of the American scene. In the opinion of some, these are significant indicators of vulnerabilities that, at the very least, impose additional claims on insufficient disposable resources, and thereby affect to some extent the allocation of resources to maintain a decently livable physical habitat.

For example, community erosion is implicit in the spreading demand for more police protection and expanding investment in protective apparatus to safeguard public and private property and to provide more personal security. Even such efforts as these, efforts that merely scratch the surface, entail substantially larger outlays of private and public funds. Comprehensive efforts to remove underlying causes would require much larger outlays. In short, we repeat, community erosion diverts attention *and money* from other urgent tasks, including environmental repair and protection.

Many scoff at the very idea of any significant erosion of the American community. Even when they recognize symptoms, most tend to deny their significance. Or if they do acknowledge some significance, they appear generally to believe that all that is required is a larger dose of chauvinistic nationalism, stronger police forces, more severe penalties for lawless violence and other offenses, and more and larger prisons to keep offenders out of circulation.

Others query such simplistic diagnoses and remedies. They sense an insidious cumulative trend into which many kinds of disruptive events seem to fit together. Anyone can compile a list of erosive symptoms from personal observations and from the daily news. Law-abiding citizens, men as well as women, especially the elderly and infirm, exhibit increasing reluctance to walk abroad at night, even in well-lighted, supposedly safe neighborhoods. Other indicators include damage to residential property even in the more "exclusive" suburbs, and everywhere seemingly unpreventable proliferation of shoplifting, burglaries, and arson, as well as ferocious robbery, mayhem, and homicide.

Whether the spread of lawless behavior is as great as the news media would have us believe, or as serious a threat to community integrity as some do firmly believe, may perhaps be debatable. What is not debatable is that these trends are nearly everywhere raising the cost of protecting person and property and thereby preempting scarce resources that might otherwise be available for other urgent purposes, including environmental protection.

Erosion of the sense of community may also weaken the will as well as the capability to cope with environmental deterioration. Stable community relationships suffer from the transient mode of life that has become the lot of millions of Americans. According to some estimates, as many as 30 to 40 million Americans move to a new address at least once every year.[19]

One recognized source of this transience is the life-style imposed by corporate managements on their executives. It used to be mainly military and foreign service officers and their families who were uprooted every two or three years by transfer to new posts. Now this gypsylike transience has become the prospect confronting thousands of corporate employees. Yanked by expediency from place to place, these potential community leaders and their families can rarely put down roots and identify with any local community.

Deploring this transience, numerous observers have asked whether American society has not already lost a sense of community. The extent to which this is literally so may be debatable, but it seems reasonable that a nation of transients, with shallow roots in the places where they temporarily reside and work, is less likely to become deeply concerned about local pollutions of air, water, and land, and other environmental problems that do initially emerge in particular municipalities, even though they may eventually reach Congress, the President, and national regulatory agencies.

A sense of community is an essential line of defense against the everyone-for-himself corollary of the exploitive marketplace ethos. As indicated in chapter 3, we find this exploitive philosophical posture to be a formidable continuing obstacle to environmental programs that curtail, or threaten to curtail, private gains, even gains that cause severe damage and hazards. That this posture exacerbates the environmental impacts of community erosion seems to us likewise probable.

The theme running through this chapter is the often neglected bearing of the structure of our domestic political and social order on the tasks of maintaining a physical habitat in which a sense of community can continue to function. The further one probes into this connection, the more apparent it becomes that progression toward higher levels and more dense industrialization have contributed in at least two ways to environmental deterioration. This progression has directly accelerated the processes of denudation, pollution, and environmental disruption. In addition, humanly dense and technically and economically complex societies proliferate vulnerabilities *that increase essential operational costs of the society and compete for the rarely adequate disposable resources needed to sustain its physical habitat.* But this is only part of the picture. In addition, the society is exposed to a varied collection of hazards that originate entirely or in part outside its geographical space, legal jurisdiction, and effective power. Some of these transnational hazards are identified in the next chapter.

∼(6)∼

Transnational Context

THIS CHAPTER enlarges the focus to include some additional conditions and forces, chiefly of foreign origin, that affect the American habitat and American responses to vulnerabilities resulting therefrom. The factors considered derive from the physical and human geography of the earth, as well as from specific policies and other activities of foreign regimes and their constituencies.

Prominent among physical features is the global unity of the natural carriers: atmosphere and seawater. These are continuously in motion. What is discharged into the atmosphere over Sinkiang, Siberia, Nevada, the South Pacific, or anywhere else, spreads over a larger area, sometimes over the entire earth. Toxic gases discharged from the chimneys of steel mills and other industrial plants drift downwind, sometimes blanketing hundreds or thousands of square miles. Building higher stacks to reduce local pollutions merely spreads the contamination over a larger area. Photographs show airborne stack-discharges drifting eastward from the Detroit area across southern Ontario and on into New York and New England. Acidic rain falls hundreds of miles from the source of the pollution. Eastward drift of polluted air from Britain has evoked complaints in Scandinavia. Radioactive fallout from weapons testing in western China shows up over the United States. Many other examples could be cited.

Seawater too circulates globally. Sewage, garbage, factory effluents, agricultural drainage, and other residues are discharged into the ocean either directly, or indirectly via inland waterways that eventually flow into the oceans and connecting seas. Whatever the source, once in the ocean these pollutants may drift with the current for hundreds or thousands of miles.

Another geographic reality is the uneven distribution of natural resources: fossil fuels and concentrated deposits of metallic and nonmetallic chemicals such as compounds of copper, iron, aluminum, sulfur, and scores of other essentials of industrial society. Still another geographical feature is the uneven distribution of renewable resources: in particular, land suitable for growing food and fiber, land that is neither too rough, too sloping, too poorly watered, too frosty, or too eroded by overcropping and other destructive farming practices.

Human geography also contributes to the transnational context of environmental politics. Countries and larger regions differ in stage of technological-economic development and hence in patterns and amounts of economic production. They differ in density of population and rates of increase, in income and wealth, in knowledge and skills, and in other social variables. By any standard one chooses, economic disparities are notorious and in the main worsening. While the rich polities are getting relatively richer, the poor (with a few exceptions) are getting relatively poorer. Their spokesmen are unreconciled to this trend and are getting plenty of publicity for their demands for a better deal than industrial imperialism has allowed them to date.

The most glaring disparities in economic and technical development are (again, with a few exceptions) between the high-income economies of the northern hemisphere and the low-income economies of the southern. The irony of this situation is accentuated by the geographical distribution of fossil fuels and many other earth materials that are more abundant in the southern hemisphere.

A geographical reality previously noted is the political fragmentation of the earth. This fragmentation into more than 145 legally sovereign polities is nearly everywhere accompanied and sustained by pervasive and persistent tribalistic attitudes that obstruct the growth of international institutions adequate to cope with the consequences of other uneven distributions.

Competitive Militarism and Transnational Violence

Military establishments are defended in terms of some definition of national security. Defense of the homeland is the one most publicized. However, military forces also serve other purposes, some of which seem to have very little to do with defense against military threats of foreign origin. Moreover, a large and expensive military establishment contributes to numerous adverse impacts on the habitat of the political community that supports it. These include preemption of material and human resources as well as direct damage to the physical habitat.

Military establishments cause environmental damage roughly in proportion to their size, cost, and level of technological sophistication. In these respects their impacts are generally similar to those of mining companies, numerous manufacturers, superhighway builders, real estate developers, agribusiness, and various other nonmilitary components of an industrial society.

In certain respects, however, military establishments cause damage and pose environmental hazards that derive from their specifically destructive missions. Operations in the war in Southeast Asia demonstrated the scale of ecological damage that military forces can inflict using herbicides, defoliants, fire, and other instruments of environmental destruction—without resort to nuclear weapons.[1]

At the level of superweapons, the enormity of hazard needs no extended elaboration here. Numerous physical scientists and others in a position to know what is yet knowable, have reiterated the monstrous hazard of abrupt environmental catastrophe inherent in possible large-scale use of thermonuclear and biochemical weapons and possibly still other military innovations.

As long as huge inventories of these superweapons exist in a world as politically volatile as ours has become, the risk of enormously destructive, possibly irreparable, disruption of the human habitat will continue to be a component of the context of environmental politics. The hazard increases with each additional hand on the nuclear trigger. It is further magnified—how much is endlessly disputed—by more or less covert research and development of chemical poisons, biological agents, and other exotic means of killing people and ruining their habitat.

Still another dimension of military-related risk lurks in research designed to achieve a capability to control weather on a regional or global scale. Such research is defended on nonmilitary grounds, and a strong prima facie case can be made for economic benefits that might accrue in particular countries or larger regions. However, ability to change climatic patterns, if achieved, would almost certainly be exploited for military purposes. It could be used to threaten and intimidate, if not actually to destroy the productive physical base, and hence the military power, of actual or putative enemies. Whether any effective defense could be invented against such a weapon is at least questionable. But it is highly probable that the geography of climatic variables would render the United States as vulnerable as any country to disruption by hostile tampering with the weather on a large scale.[2]

Climatic manipulation is but one of the means by which military-related science and engineering contribute to harmful changes in the physical habitat. A 1976 report listed nineteen more or less distinct "environmental modification techniques, designed to achieve para-military objectives." These included tampering with the land, ocean, and atmosphere.[3]

Whether these and other advances in the covert and violent arts of environmental as well as human destruction are decreasing or increasing the security of the American republic in any meaningful sense is at least debatable. However, the possibility of abrupt irreversible catastrophe by military and military-related means should not simply be swept under the carpet. Regimes that deploy today's, and are preparing tomorrow's, superweapons can probably destroy the civilization and habitability of any country, and just possibly the entire biosphere.

Such a capability can be maintained only at an economic cost that profoundly affects the allocation of intellectual and physical resources.[4] Mid-nineteenth-century British governments defended their homeland, policed a global empire, and exerted on other nations an influence at least as great as the United States achieved briefly in the 1950s and 1960s. The British did this at a real cost of not more than one or two percent of the military budgets of the United States in recent years.[5] This comparison draws attention not only to the self-limiting benefits of competitive militarism in our era but also to the ruinous economic cost of this risky game. Military establishments have become voracious, insatiable consumers of energy, materials, productive capital, managerial skills, and scientific and engineering research.

This preemption is magnified by production of weapons and military-related equipment for export. Hard data regarding this international traffic are difficult to obtain. International sales of military equipment from developed to developing countries are estimated to have totaled $300 millions in 1952, and $19 *billions* in 1974, an increase of 6,000 percent in twenty-two years, in addition to massive supplements of other military-related transactions. The Stockholm International Peace Research Institute (SIPRI) estimates that the value of global traffic in arms is "running at about $20 billions" annually, and that total world military expenditures reached about $280 billions in 1975 alone.

American participation in this exploding traffic in arms exceeds that of all competitors. SIPRI reported that in 1975 American producers held outstanding orders totaling $35.5 billions and delivered goods worth nearly $16 billions. Production for export, plus allocations to the American military establishment, has preempted energy, materials, industrial capital, and manpower on a colossal scale. This commitment includes scientific and engineering personnel, alone estimated to "equal 40 percent of the world's most qualified scientists and engineers."[6]

The export of military hardware is defended as a necessary contribution to balance the international accounts of the American economy. This claim may or may not be tenable if all other relevant factors and possibilities are taken into account. What is not debatable is that the American military establishment and America's share in the international arms traffic preempt vast quantities of resources, at least some of which could otherwise be allocated to constructive social programs, and also to getting on with the task of arresting progressive deterioration of the American physical habitat.

In this broader context, it is relevant to query whether governmental appropriations for military and military-related purposes that preempt a quarter to a third of American federal revenues, and around 6 percent of the GNP, may not themselves become a major source of vulnerability to the society and habitat which the military establishment is maintained to defend. We would venture still further a tentative conjecture that no economy—American, Soviet, nor any other—can continue much longer to pay so high a price for an elusive military primacy without progressively weakening the domestic society and physical habitat—the productive bases from which all military establishments derive their power and credibility.

To suggest this conclusion is not to attack the legitimacy of military defense. Anyone can verify our well-known position on this issue by consulting previous writings. Our purpose here is simply to focus attention on hidden costs and environmentally harmful by-products of contemporary competitive militarism. Whether what is gained compensates for the price paid in societal erosion and environmental degradation seems to us a relevant question. Moreover, it is a question unanswerable by conventional benefit-cost calculations.

A spin-off from military production is the expanding international commerce in nuclear technology, reactors, and fuels. Regarding the latter, William Epstein (formerly director of the Armaments Division of the United Nations) listed twenty-five governments that in 1975 were contemplating early development of nuclear power facilities, or actually negotiating with American, French, German, or other suppliers. Exports of nuclear technology and equipment, for purposes asserted to be purely peaceful, are defended as useful instruments of foreign policy, as legitimate business, and as an important contribution to fuller employment within the United States. However, as Epstein observes, "There is no essential technological difference between a nuclear explosive intended for peaceful purposes and one intended for waging war."[7]

Proliferation of nuclear capabilities further expands opportunities for foreign governmental pressures, and even blackmail, against the suppliers of the hardware and its technology. In particular it becomes, at least potentially, a significant factor in the intensifying demands of many LDC regimes for a much larger share of the world's developed wealth and for more favorable terms of trade for their fossil fuels, essential minerals, and such consumer items as coffee.

The combination of nuclear proliferation, conventional arms traffic, electronic communications, and high mobility of goods and personnel provides a brew that enlarges the opportunities for transnational extension of the terrorist activities described in the preceding chapter. In one hypothetical example, it is noted that a terrorist operation could now "be planned in Germany by a Palestine Arab, executed in Israel by terrorists recruited in Japan, with weapons acquired in Italy but manufactured in Russia, supplied by an Algerian diplomat financed with Libyan money."[8]

The bearing of terrorism on future relations between the high-income industrial polities and the low-income LDCs is gradually getting more attention. Mihajlo Mesarovic and Eduard Pestel are among those who take this magnified threat seriously. They plead for a "more equitable long-term allocation" of energy and other resources. They emphasize, in particular, the shortage of fossil fuels and urge curtailment of "further overdevelopment" of the industrialized regions, by the acceptance of "limits on per-capita use of finite resources." They warn that "unless this lesson is learned in time, there will be a thousand desperadoes terrorizing those who are now 'rich,' and eventually nuclear blackmail and terror will paralyze further orderly development."[9]

Contemplating this prospect, the nuclear physicist Bernard Feld envisions relative security attainable only by an "iron-clad system of control over plutonium stores—preferably an international agency—to ensure that under no reasonably conceivable circumstances could they fall into irresponsible hands." Then he adds a caveat of the greatest importance: "This situation presumes a degree of international control over a vital source of economic power that has no precedent in history." [10]

From another informed speaker comes a similar premonition, and some salient advice: "The trend toward nuclear power may be inevitable. But we, and the rest of the world, ought to know now what we are letting ourselves in for." [11]

What is hinted at is that we in the high-income industrialized societies may be letting ourselves in for the fate envisioned by Mesarovic and Pestel. It may or may not happpen; but it is already evident that the minimal prospect is for indefinitely rising outlays for protection—to the extent that protection against international terrorism is attainable at any price in the current disturbed state of the world. Furthermore, *such extra costs will inexorably compete with social and environmental and still other demands for the chronically insufficient resources at the disposal of our public authorities.*

Threats from the Third World

We have noted the increasing leverage of some of the LDCs through their sovereignty over dwindling reserves of fossil fuels and other high-grade natural resources. Any serious consideration of this leverage should include some of the responses available to the larger importers of these industrial essentials. Such consideration should include transnational effects that derive, or may yet derive, from differences among countries in permitted levels of industrial pollutions. It should also include the stiffening competition for energy and raw materials that seems inevitable to the extent that industrial development actually gains momentum in the Third World.

On the first issue, one encounters differences in the conjectures of specialists, especially economists. Many envision dependence on undependable foreign sources of fuels and raw materials as a temporary risk that can be eradicated, or greatly reduced, within a decade or two by technological innovations and a freer market.

A different view is expressed by another economist, C. Fred Bergsten, who has given much attention to this issue. "The United States is rapidly joining the rest of the industrialized countries in depending on the Third World for a critical share of its energy supplies and other natural resources." In addition to the international oil cartel, Bergsten envisions the possibility of similar constraints on transnational commerce by international organizations of producers of copper, tin, natural rubber, bauxite, coffee, timber, and numerous other commodities.

Rulers of producing countries, he continues, "could exercise maximum leverage through withholding supplies altogether, at least from a single customer such as the United States." Or they could "charge higher prices for their raw materials, directly or through such techniques as insisting that they process the materials themselves. . . . Such Third World leverage could have a double bite on the United States if used discriminatorily."[12]

Economist Ragaei Mallakh supports Bergsten's argument with statistics showing that the American economy already depends on foreign supplies for 90 percent of its bauxite, 80 percent of its tin, 80 percent of its nickel, nearly 100 percent of its chromium, 95 percent of its manganese, and 30 percent of its iron ore. He predicts that these import-percentages "will rise in coming years if only to maintain our present level of industrial requirements."[13]

What kinds of responses to such pressures would be feasible and effective? This question has evoked numerous suggestions. A recurring theme is the need for more cooperation by the industrial high-income polities against the producers of oil and other industrial essentials. Another is the demand for retaliatory denial, or curtailment, of aid to those countries, especially technical assistance, industrial equipment, and (in certain cases) even food to relieve famine. A third suggestion is to take by force what the producers of energy and essential minerals refuse to sell, or will sell only at inflated prices. A fourth is to reduce

American dependence on imports of oil and other imported essentials by subsidizing exploitation of domestic sources. A fifth, rarely considered seriously as yet, is to narrow the still-widening gap in per capita income between rich and poor countries along lines proposed by Mesarovic and Pestel and others. A sixth suggestion, even less seriously considered until the long cold winter of 1976–1977 and the inauguration of the Carter administration, is to reduce drastically the waste of fuels, electric power, and imported materials—waste which contributes substantially to shortages and rising prices of supplies. All such proposals pose unresolved problems regarding probable effectiveness and political prudence as well as economic costs and risks involved.

Another envisaged source of vulnerability, largely conjectural as of 1977, derives from differences in permitted levels of industrial pollution. In virtually all the LDCs the drive to industrialize takes precedence over long-range hazards. It is widely reported that smoking industrial chimneys are regarded in those countries as indicators of progress rather than portents of future disasters. It is also reported that some of the LDCs welcome high-polluting industries seeking a haven from tightening standards in the United States.

We have heard numerous Americans contend that this way of exporting pollution to the Third World offers a cheap and satisfactory solution for some of our own confrontations between industrial managements and environmental activists. This attitude reflects the myopic vision that prevents so many people in so many countries from comprehending the extent to which environmental degradation in one country produces adverse effects in others, sooner or later. Moreover even moderate tightening of antipollution controls within the United States without concurrent tightening in other countries imposes a more or less onerous handicap—in some instances a severe burden—on American industries.

The economist Marshall Goldman compares such tactics to the working of Gresham's often quoted "law" of money. Just as "bad money tends to drive good money out of circulation, so poor pollution control tends to drive out good pollution control, or at least makes it harder to enact good environmental law." [14]

It will take time and more evidence to demonstrate how serious this threat may become. It is not a simple operation to move major industries. Many considerations enter into corporate decisions to move or stay put. Not least is the political climate of pollution-tolerant LDCs. However, it is credible that some industries may move to more permissive environments, and that charges of unfair competition will make it even more difficult to enact and enforce antipollution standards within the United States.

Efforts to persuade leaders of the LDCs that tolerance of industrial pollution is short-sighted and may be self-destructive in the longer run have accomplished little to date. The outlook seems to be pretty much as anticipated in 1970 by a panel on "implications of change," in the Massachusetts Institute of Technology's reconnaissance of "critical environmental problems." That panel found "little reason to believe that the developing countries can be diverted from their preoccupation with the first-order effects of technology to a concern about the side effects upon the environment. Currently, and in the foreseeable future, the advanced industrial societies will have to carry the load of remedial action against pollution." [15]

Finally, to the extent that industrialization does make headway in the LDCs, they will become progressively stronger competitors with the already industrialized economies for larger shares of accessible energy, metals, and other materials upon which industrialism feeds. The entry of these new claimants into international markets will coincide with still rising demands from the older industrialized societies, if the needs of the latter continue to expand as some optimists predict.

The prospect that emerges from these concurrent trends is further accelerative depletion of accessible high-grade natural resources. At the very least, if this scenario materializes, competition seems certain to drive still higher the already high prices of energy and numerous other industrial essentials. At worst, it might shorten radically the reprieve for orderly adjustment from the waning era of abundance for a few nations to an era of multiplying scarcities for all.[16]

Prior to the Arab oil embargo, much of the discussion of energy and other resources proceeded as if the Third World did not exist, or as if the LDCs could do nothing that would significantly threaten the flow of cheap energy and materials to the high-income parts of the world. The 1973–1974 crisis advertised the extent to which Asian, African, and Latin American regimes with little or no power in the traditional sense could harass the economies of the industrial giants.

We conclude this section by suggesting a tentative hypothesis: Under emerging conditions, the United States and other large consumers of imported energy and materials are confronted with at least three unpleasant options. One is to strive for higher-cost self-sufficiency, an objective possibly unattainable at current and anticipated levels of consumption, and certain to deplete still more rapidly their own exploitable domestic reserves. A second is to accept higher-risk and higher-cost dependence upon imports from the LDCs. A third option is multinational cooperation that goes far beyond anything as yet seriously considered toward sharing, and hence redistributing, income and wealth in order to meet at least partway the demands of the low-income majority of the inchoate world community.[17]

Insidious Intruders

We come next to a varied assortment of intruders that penetrate the tightest quarantines and the most heavily guarded political borders. These unwelcome intruders include pollutants transported around the world by the great natural carriers: wind and seawater. Others—especially pathogenic organisms—penetrate every country as stowaways in the goods of commerce and in the luggage and bodies of international travelers.

Before going further, it should be emphasized that not all pollutants are transnational migrants. However, strictly local pollutions may entail international consequences. Noise around airports is a local phenomenon. Refusal to grant landing permits to excessively noisy foreign planes has become an international political issue. Likewise, reducing legal highway speed to conserve energy and lessen hazards is prima facie a purely domestic question, but it may produce transnational consequences, such as angry protests from foreign governments whose speeding diplomats are escorted off the turnpikes by police.

Polluted boundary lakes and rivers have long been a persistent if relatively minor source of international concern. We have noted that air pollution in one country may drift downwind into others. Scientists and others involved in weapons testing, as well as those involved in expansion of a nuclear-fission power industry, have minimized the risk to vegetation, animals, and humans. But well-informed counterjudgments are reflected in demands for more effective worldwide monitoring and effective safeguards which if achieved will add substantially to the ever-expanding costs of maintaining a viable international order and habitat.

Another form of insidious intrusion would be damage, possibly irreversible damage, from long-term changes in global climates. Such changes might result from events in outer space, or in nonhuman phenomena of terrestrial nature—or they might be deliberate or unanticipated consequences of human activities. In any case, there seems to be nearly a scientific consensus that major changes in climate could not be contained within the geographic space of a single country, and that some would suffer very adverse changes in weather.

Still another category of insidious intruders includes the countless viruses, bacteria, parasites, fungi, and insects that migrate from country to country. These migrants injure or destroy plants, animals, and humans. They filter through all protective barriers yet invented. Their potential for damage has risen with the expansion of intercountry commerce and travel. The economic damage *and costs* inflicted by such migrants as the Mediterranean fruit fly, Japanese beetle, fire ant, gypsy moth, and a vast assortment of other pests need no elaboration here.

The fragile defenses against such pests as these and against those that attack humans directly are costly and only partially effective.

Even greater hazards lurk in genetic research and experimentation. No one has plausibly rebutted warnings of eminent scientists that this agenda entails risk of worldwide epidemics traceable to the escape from some laboratory of a newly invented pathogen for which no therapy is available.

We have heard it argued that public expenditures for protection against destructive organisms and other migratory hazards are only a tiny fraction of the national product. Such arguments usually fail to take into account the private costs, both economic and pathological. The total costs that these insidious migrants inflict—in human morbidity and mortality, in pesticides and crop losses, in monitoring, inspection, quarantine, immunization, medical research, and other health services—*add substantial increments to the steadily accelerating price of protection against the multiple vulnerabilities to which contemporary Americans are continuously and increasingly exposed.*

The Tragedy of the Oceanic Commons

The international public domains present additional sources of damage and risk. These are areas outside the legal jurisdiction of *any* sovereign state. They are somewhat analogous to the public domains of domestic law: areas or other benefits which individuals and organizations are legally entitled to use, but in principle only in ways that do not significantly degrade the domain in question or injure others who are entitled to share fairly in benefits derived therefrom.

The international public domains consist mainly of the following areas: the "high sea"—those parts of the global ocean and its connecting seas over which no state can legally claim exclusive jurisdiction; less explicitly, the polar regions; and still more vaguely, the stratosphere and outer space. With respect to all these areas, national rights of access and exploitation are partially delineated by traditional international law and treaties.

However, there are substantial legal gaps in which generally accepted rules define vaguely, or not at all, the limits of legitimate national use and exploitation.

The doctrine of fair access and exploitation has historical antecedents—among others, the concept of the "commons" in English law. This principle arose in connection with use of land within and around rural villages in medieval England. The essence of the principle was that some of the land was more or less permanently assigned to particular individuals, called "commoners," but the rest was held "in common" by the village, and made available to villagers in accord with rather complicated rules regarding permissible use. The basic principle was that the "commoner could turn out [into the common land] as many head of cattle as he could keep by means of the lands that were parcelled out to him." [18]

The right of the commons was susceptible to abuse. It was in part a sort of honor system, based upon requisites more or less analogous to those that sustain an examination honor system in a few American colleges. The system worked, as well as it did, to the extent that individuals conformed to the rules, whether from moral rectitude and stern conscience or from the social pressures of watchful fellow commoners in a tightly knit community from which an offender had no easy avenue of escape. [19]

A few years ago the American biologist Garrett Hardin used this historic analogy to explain why, in his judgment, it is futile to depend on voluntary conformity to arrest progressive degradation of the biosphere. He calls the failure of voluntarism the "tragedy of the commons." There is plenty of evidence to support a prima facie case for Hardin's thesis: in particular, exploitive national policies and practices that deplete, pollute, and ecologically disrupt the international ocean. That is to say, the tragedy of the oceanic commons is the almost universal propensity to put short-term personal or corporate or governmental objectives ahead of long-term human values in this immense domain.

World maps designate five oceans and numerous connecting seas. In the aggregate these contain about 300 million cubic miles of seawater and cover about 70 percent of the earth's surface. This global ocean is a diluted source of nearly all inert resources upon or beneath the land's surface or in the atmosphere. The ocean is also the habitat of organisms that release, via photosynthesis, much of the free oxygen that enables oxygen-breathing organisms to survive.

Garbage, sewage, industrial effluents, spilled oil, and other noxious residues of the earth's expanding human population, progressively contaminate the global ocean. Some of this pollution is biodegradable, but apparently not enough. There is evidence of progressive contamination of the oceanic commons, with accompanying damage to aquatic organisms that absorb solar energy and transmute some of it into free oxygen.

Pollutants also contaminate aquatic organisms without killing them outright. Poisonous chemicals ingested by microscopic plankton are transmitted upward through food chains. Some of these poisons eventually reach the dinner tables of rich and poor alike, either as contaminated fish and other seafood, or less directly via food animals fed on fish meal and other products of the sea.

Disruption of photosynthesis and direct damage to human health from marine pollution are only parts of a larger picture. Another part is the accelerative exploitation of the oceans and seas for food. Except for a few species, risk of extermination is still an issue in controversy. But there are indications that machine-intensive fishing as practiced by the Soviet Union, Japan, Norway, Canada, and a few other states, with electronic apparatus to locate the fish and floating factories to process the catch, is progressively reducing a number of the more important food species.

The oceans are also a source—still only a potential source, in the main—of industrial materials. These are generally expensive to recover and require complex equipment and techniques. But oceanic resources are becoming more coveted as high-grade resources extractable from the land become progressively depleted and lower-grade materials command higher prices. Numerous reservoirs of oil beneath the continental shelves have already been tapped, with further more difficult and expensive drilling and pumping operations projected or in course of development. Concentrated manganese and other essential minerals have been discovered in the deeper seabed, sometimes far from the coast, and additional discoveries are anticipated with introduction of still more sophisticated apparatus. Seawater itself contains in solution minute quantities of virtually every mineral that exists in nature. Evidence to date indicates that attempts at recovery of these minerals will bring a high probability of greatly increased pollution resulting from accidents and other causes, and, in varying degrees, ancillary damage to adjacent shores.

According to traditional law, jurisdiction of maritime states extends only a limited distance from the coast. The historic limit was 3 miles. During the past half-century, more and more governments have unilaterally claimed jurisdiction to 12 or more miles. Today, numerous governments (including that of the United States) are asserting jurisdiction as far as 200 miles from shore. The main objective is to maximize the area reserved for national exploitation, with or without regard to sustaining the ecology of the ocean.

This is a trend that discriminates to the advantage of states with longer seacoasts; and in this respect, the United States is well situated. The trend also favors national economies that command the complex technology and abundant energy required to exploit the continental shelf and the ocean depths— again a condition that favors the short-term interests of American corporations and the United States government.

Whether, on balance, longer-term interests will be ignored, as in so many other areas, by extending to the global ocean the political fragmentation that prevails upon the land is more debatable. Overfishing manifestly cannot continue indefinitely. Continued use of the oceans as the ultimate cesspool portends in the long run a habitat less congenial for humans everywhere. Progressive contamination of the oceanic food chains exposes humans to a variety of risks as yet imperfectly understood. At worst, numerous scientists seem convinced, there is genuine risk that disruption of the complex ecology of the ocean may insidiously disrupt the total ecology of the earth as a whole. Be all this as it may, the fact remains that so far nearly all efforts to cope with the tragedy of the oceanic commons have foundered on the rocks of national sovereignty and diminishing accessible resources from other sources.

In the foregoing pages, we have omitted the centuries-old intermittent struggles to achieve military control of some or all of the global ocean. Traditional international law legitimizes control of the "high sea" by any regime that can assemble sufficient military force to achieve it. For a few decades in the nineteenth century the British navy came rather close to achieving a global "command of the seas" against all putative enemies. Today the oceans and connecting seas have reverted to an arena of competitive militarism, in which nuclear-powered submarines as well as surface craft and airplanes, armed with thermonuclear missiles, add a further increment to the presumptive capability of at least two governments—American and Russian—to bring disruption of the physical habitat to an abrupt, possibly terminal, climax.

～(7)～

"No Free Lunch"
The Costs of Environmental Protection

ONE OF THE few issues on which ecology and conventional economic theory seem to be generally in accord is that there is "no free lunch": environmental protection always carries a price tag.

It seems fairly obvious that protection against harmful conditions or changes in the physical habitat entails costs that someone has to pay, whether in money or in some other currency. Hence, environmental costs are important ingredients of the context of environmental politics: that is, these costs affect what and how much is undertaken toward redressing damage incurred and reducing risks of future damage.

An essential preliminary is to clarify what such costs include. The reference may be to the monetary cost of redressing damage to the extent that redress is possible. Or cost may refer to the estimated dollar-price of eradicating or reducing a specified hazard—that is, coping with a source of future damage. Estimates of costs vary widely, depending on what items are included. Calculations exclusively in monetary units nearly always omit costs that are not meaningfully measurable in such units. Consider a hypothetical case: the costs of building and operating a coal-fired power plant. Plainly, space here is insufficient to cover all items, but enough perhaps to indicate the scope and complexity of cost analysis.

Construction of the plant consumes energy and materials, including outlays for their transportation and for design, direction, labor, and other items. Some of these operations produce residues that pollute air, water, and land. Most of the environmentally linked costs of construction are measurable in dollars. However, in the course of construction, workers are injured or killed. The cost of death is impossible, and of disablement difficult, to measure in money.

Operation of the plant consumes large quantities of fuel. Extracting the coal from mines presents further hazards to life and health. Through time, the fuel consumed also depletes by so much the recoverable reserves remaining in the earth. The mining process itself consumes energy made available by other energy-consuming operations—and so on, ad infinitum. Most but not all of these items are calculable in monetary units.

Sometimes, as described in chapter 4, the cost of developing a new energy source, or continuing to exploit a developed source, approaches the units of energy of the additional energy made available. The higher the cost in terms of energy consumption, the lower the profits of the whole operation. This is stated to be one of the reasons why oil-bearing shale in our mountain states and tar sands in western Canada have so far failed to attract sufficient capital for large-scale development. It is also one of the reasons why direct exploitation of solar energy in large quantities is slow in developing; why nuclear-fission power plants may produce considerably less net energy than their advocates anticipate; and why nuclear fusion may never pay its way in net energy produced even if the technical obstacles are overcome. That is, as we have emphasized in chapter 4, it takes energy to get energy; and directly or indirectly private consumers pay in prices or in taxes for every BTU consumed, including the energy consumed in the process of making more energy available.

In our illustrative example, the mined coal must be transported to the power plant, another energy-consuming process. At the plant it is burned to produce steam to drive the generators, a process that is never 100-percent efficient, and hence entails further loss of energy. The mining process produces slack, and the burning at the plant produces additional wastes, chiefly ashes. Both of these by-products pollute land, and sometimes water and air in addition. Reduction of such pollutions entails further energy expenditures. Failure to reduce this pollution produces mental and physical suffering that adversely affects all members of the community. Reduction of this pollution requires treatment that consumes still more energy, measurable in dollars or in dollar-equivalents of BTUs.

Among direct effects of these pollutions may be included damage to commercial crops grown in the vicinity and to private gardens and ornamental plantings. Various indirect consequences may follow, such as aesthetic revulsion, property depreciation, physiological injuries to wildlife and humans, and other ramifying corollaries of the "no free lunch" proposition.

Anyone can draw on his observations for other examples of the weblike tangle of depletions, pollutions, and disruptions, and the monetary and other costs that these entail. Such interactions are occurring everywhere in varying patterns. In the aggregate, depending on the density of population, level of technological-economic development, average material standard of living, and other variables, these interactions produce environmental changes that are economically ruinous to some, aesthetically objectionable to others, and pathologically injurious to many, whether or not the affected individuals comprehend what is happening to them until it is too late to matter.

Any of these three kinds of changes—depletions, pollutions, disruptions—may be harmful, often severely harmful. Further expenditures of energy and materials are usually required to compensate for damage incurred and to eradicate or reduce sources of future damage. Energy and materials, research, direction, labor, are all involved—and someone has to pay the bills.

As previously emphasized, dysfunctional changes in the habitat become "live" problems only when private individuals or groups, or public authorities representing the community as a whole, recognize that significant damage is being incurred, or that substantial risk is imminent. The outcome may be a decision to do nothing or something. Doing nothing usually transfers the cost to future consumers and taxpayers, possibly to those still unborn. Or the decision may be to refrain from doing something. Leaving the coal in the ground would be an example of such a response. Or the response may be positive, such as changing a process to reduce pollution. Either refraining from use or regulating use is nearly certain to entail still further costs that show up in private and public accounts, and ultimately in taxes and commodity prices.

The conclusion toward which this argument is heading is that virtually anything done to increase supplies and consumption produces pollutions, and that the end result is a less safe and healthful habitat, unless still further costs are incurred. Procrastination may entail additional costs. Increasing rates of depletion, involving many different resources, are nearly certain to worsen serious ecological disruptions that increase still further the eventual costs of environmental repair and protection. In a still longer view, some well-informed experts envision continued accelerative disruption culminating in various kinds of disasters, reparable if at all by economic outlays and altered modes of living as yet only roughly conjectural.

The above example and comments, though fragmentary and oversimplified, indicate that estimating costs of preventing and repairing harmful environmental impacts is a complex and tricky business; and one should never forget that some estimators play tricks on the ill-informed or unwary.

One precaution against being taken in by incomplete or deceptive estimates is to understand what can and what cannot be learned from conventional benefit-cost formulas and calculations. Such formulas are expressed in the vernacular of economics. One is told that a cleaner, quieter, safer, and more healthful environment will cost some estimated number of dollars. A corollary (not always mentioned) is that the burden is certain to be distributed unevenly among different categories of income receivers. Something (likewise expressed in monetary units) will have to be given up in return, unless per capita income of the community is rising sufficiently to cover the additional costs. Since there is "no free lunch" there will have to be trade-offs between what is gained and what is lost.

Rarely, if ever, do the promoters of large projects calculate and include all the costs, even those that are more or less measurable in monetary units. Consider the case of Egypt's Aswan Dam. Garrett Hardin tells what happened: "There was a study of a sort," but it was purely economic and myopic at that. "There was no mention of the costs of a new fertilizer industry, of a far-flung medical program, of a soil reclamation program, or of developing a new occupation for displaced fishermen, and nothing at all about controlling pathological processes in the body politic. . . . What was missing in the preliminary cost-benefit analysis was the ecologic view. The analysis was merely economic, in the narrowest sense."[1]

All major undertakings and many minor ones present comparably complex environmentally linked costs. People should become more sensitive to such questions as: How does one determine the dollar value of better health and longer life for coal miners against the cost of making mines safer and more healthful places to work? How is one to weigh in dollars the cost of devising and installing less deadening factory routines against the price of automobiles? How express in dollars the psychological benefits of cleaner air and less noise against the taxes and commodity prices paid to achieve such intangible benefits?

Two other complications arise: first, trying to apply conventional benefit-cost formulas to changes in the habitat that may not severely injure people currently living, but pose a threat of serious defects in the newborn; and second, trying to calculate the dollar-cost of burdens and hazards that extend beyond the life-span of those doing the calculating. In short, conventional benefit-cost analysis omits a battery of ethical questions that are simply swept under the carpet.

Consider the following illustrative question: *Should* the United States government impose severe penalties for gross waste of energy, or try to evade the question by subsidizing massive development of a nuclear-fission power industry in the face of

credible warnings from many different sources that illicit interventions, human failures, and technical malfunctions present
formidable hazards that might cover large geographic areas and
kill or injure millions of people? And the further question:
Should currently living policymakers burden future generations,
perhaps for thousands of years, with lethal hazards from radio-
activity leaking from obsolete reactors, spent fuels, and other
residues of nuclear power development?

Now, consider another example: Many biochemists believe
that they are getting close to the capability of creating new life
forms—including previously unknown viruses and bacteria,
and even more complex organisms. Enthusiastic advocates of
this research agenda predict immense potential for producing
a "better" environment for humans. But other scientists, comparably well informed, view this agenda with mounting alarm.
They emphasize that no one knows what collateral consequences as well as direct results may occur: what known diseases may become more virulent, what new diseases may
emerge, what uncontrollable epidemics may wipe out entire
populations, what noxious plants and animals, or even humanlike monsters, may eventually be created.

In short, here is a research agenda with claimed beneficial
potential, but also vast potentials for disaster, possibly including
destruction of the human species.[2] Should public authorities
permit, not to mention support, such a risky business?

Let us ask some further questions about the moral/ethical as
well as economic hazards that confront the cost calculator. What
objectives should be envisioned with reference to pollutions of
air, water, and land? Reduction only of those that are physiologically disabling to everyone concerned? Should the objectives
include reduction of noise? Protection of workers in mines and
factories, on mechanized farms, and in other dangerous working places? Regulation and enforcement of safety and health
standards in slaughterhouses, dairies, bakeries, and other food-
handling plants? Protection of wildlife by restrictions on pesticides? Preservation of landscapes that evoke aesthetic pleasure

in some if not all observers? Protection of all ecological systems that affect human well-being?

Manifestly, dollar costs will vary widely depending on what is included or omitted.

Costs also depend on the level of standards prescribed, and quality standards likewise depend on choices among competing demands. For example, *how much* air pollution should be tolerated? Should the standard be high enough to protect infants, elderly folk, and persons with special vulnerabilities (such as cardiac and lung disabilities, for example)? Or low enough to protect only "normal healthy" young and middle-aged adults?

How much raw sewage should municipalities be allowed to discharge into public water sources? *How much* toxic waste from industrial plants? Should the permissible level be low enough to protect trout and other aquatic organisms that require relatively clean, oxygen-rich water? Low enough to protect commercial fisheries only? Low enough to keep bathing beaches safe for vacationers? *Should* certain waterways be deliberately allowed to degrade into more or less permanent open sewers, as has been repeatedly suggested for Lake Erie and numerous major rivers?

How much noise should be tolerated in city streets, in factories, and around airports? Should prevention of pathological deafness be the only criterion? Or should emotional impacts of excessive noise also be considered? Or should reduction of noise be ignored on the premise that all industrial societies are incurably noisy?

Should public policy ignore rising food prices attributed to restricting the use of nonbiodegradable pesticides? Higher prices for lumber resulting from restricted timber cutting in wilderness preserves? Higher prices for coal and electric power from enforcing higher safety standards in mines and power plants? Higher prices for heating oil and motor fuel and other petroleum products from restricting imports? What trade-offs should be taken into consideration between predominantly aesthetic values and business profits? Whose values? Whose profits? What trade-offs should regulations embody between better health for millions and the continued flow of luxuries to a few thousands? What preferences should be given to the poor at the expense of the rich—and vice versa? Merely to ask such questions reveals the nonsense characteristic of many so-called benefit-cost assertions.

In every instance above, the words *should* and *how much* signal an ethical choice; such choices are not, and cannot be, meaningfully expressed exclusively or even primarily in monetary units, or resolved by conventional benefit-cost formulas and calculations. In the final reckoning, as argued from the first page of this book, strategies for dealing with pollutions of air and with other sources of vulnerability from conditions and changes in the physical habitat turn on ethical as well as technical and economic criteria. That is to say, they include *choices among values* that cannot be measured in the currency of the marketplace and defy quantification.[3]

We are not suggesting that the economic ingredients of environmental costs are negligible, trivial, or irrelevant. Quite the contrary: In many instances, the dollar costs of eradicating or reducing environmentally associated risks can be estimated more or less credibly, given necessary information which unfortunately is not always available. Such knowledge, however, while decidedly relevant, is by itself generally insufficient. Authoritative decisions—to do nothing or something, and if the latter, what and how much—are always taken within some frame of priorities that includes an ethical/moral element.

On this issue Allen V. Kneese, an economist who has given much study to the question of environmental costs, seems to us to be on firm ground when he affirms that "benefit-cost analysis can supply useful inputs to the political process for making policy decisions, but it cannot begin to provide a complete answer, especially to questions with such far-reaching implications for society."[4]

There have been scores if not hundreds of environmental cost estimates. Most of these cover only particular projects and operations, such as, say, sanitizing municipal sewage before permitting discharge into waterways or upon the land. Other estimates are more comprehensive. All are based on some set of quality standards. A few estimators have attempted (fruitlessly, in our judgment) to assign monetary values to ethical preferences at the core of environmental policymaking. Though published estimates vary widely, most of the more comprehensive ones seem to envisage outlays approaching the cost of conducting an endless major war upon the opposite side of our planet.[5]

Costs of such magnitude would not cripple the American economy, as some pessimists have contended. Nor would they necessarily curtail reasonable economic growth. But it does seem likely that a comprehensive program of environmental repair and protection would entail major changes in the structure of the economy, at least some changes in the distribution of private income and wealth, and in the uses to which spendable income could be put.

It is naïve to assume, as many have done, that environmental costs will necessarily, or even probably, be absorbed by those primarily responsible for wasteful consumption of energy and materials and for major pollutions and ecological disruptions— even if such costs are charged directly to the wasters and polluters. Nor does it seem realistic to anticipate that very many private enterprises, municipalities, even federal agencies, will absorb large extra costs entailed in changing their modes of operation.

If environmental costs are paid largely in the form of charges, or taxes, on polluting industries, some or all of this will be passed along to consumers in higher prices for food, clothing, housing, fuel and power, automobiles, household equipment, and most other items of personal consumption. As previously noted, any such mode of financing environmental repair and protection seems likely to be as regressive as the flat-rate sales taxes that discriminate against the society's lower-income receivers.

If environmental costs are paid largely from public funds, who pays—and how much—will depend on the sources of governmental revenue: if from state and local flat-rate sales and property taxes, the middle- and lower-income classes will carry the heavier burden; if from revenues on income, the burden will shift somewhat toward the higher income brackets.

Though we have not ignored microenvironments in this discussion of costs, the emphasis has been mainly on conditions and changes in macroenvironments. Costs have been considered in rather general terms, with only occasional references to the specific places where people live, work, and play. Costs associated with improvement of these microenvironments are not negligible, and they too keep rising as legislative bodies and the courts extend the principle of public and private liability for injuries incurred in dangerous situations: requiring, for example, compensation to workers for illness incurred by breathing toxic chemicals in poorly ventilated mines and factories, or compensation for injuries attributable to inadequately maintained rental premises. From such extensions of the right of personal redress for environmentally related injuries, it would not require a very long leap to extend public liability for damage to private property from industry-derived acidic rainfall or other dysfunctional conditions in local as well as larger environments. In short, it requires no great stretch of imagination to envisage progressive extensions of liability—both public and private—for damage to specific individuals as well as to communities, from a lengthening list of harmful conditions and changes in the physical habitat.

Most of this is conjectural as yet. But the extensions of private and public liability (with concomitant increase of costs) that have occurred within the past generation or so would have seemed as improbable to mid-nineteenth-century Victorians as the conjectures above probably seem to most Americans today. However, potentialities for such extensions of liability and costs are clearly present in our contemporary milieu; and the velocity of change may already be greater than is generally appreciated. The rationale for this conjecture, and some of the consequences implicit therein, provide the main focus of the next chapter.

~(8)~

Costs, Resources, & Priorities

The Statesmen's Dilemma

PROLIFERATING demands from many diverse sources' enlarge the share of the national income, and hence of corporate and personal incomes, which is taken by government through taxation and other means, and then allocated by public authorities according to some schedule of priorities. This process makes governmental budgets increasingly revealing indicators of changes in priorities between environmental objectives and a multiplicity of other claims that derive from chronic poverty and discrimination amidst affluence, from the costs of competitive militarism, and from various other sources.

Several years ago we suggested calling this complex phenomenon "the dilemma of rising demands and insufficient resources."[1] Here we call it simply the statesmen's dilemma, even though it is only one of numerous dilemmas that beset public authorities at every level of government.

Resources at the disposal of rulers have rarely seemed to them sufficient for their purposes. Allocations to claimants have just as rarely satisfied the latter. What is relatively new, and extremely important in the present context, is the concurrence of conditions that pose this ancient dilemma in an especially intractable form, particularly in industrial urban societies, and above all in the United States. Here, as in numerous countries, an unremitting contest for larger shares of insufficient disposable resources has become a persistent ingredient of the context of environmental politics.

The dilemma of insufficient disposable resources derives from numerous conditions, some of which are especially constrictive in the United States. One of these is the deeply rooted expectation of perpetually expanding opportunity and increasing material affluence. This expectation has been characterized as a built-in feature of American culture.[2] A large minority of Americans have shared only marginally in the amenities to which scores of millions have become habituated. However, despite doubts here and there, public expectation of perpetually expanding goods and services seems to be as firmly entrenched as ever.

As noted in chapter 3, this expectation is built not only into personal images of the future but also into technocratic and conventional economic theories. It is assumed by architects of party platforms, highway planners, automobile and other manufacturers, real estate developers, military planners, and virtually everyone else involved in the production or consumption of goods and services.[3]

Warnings and supporting evidence that our planet is being acceleratively stripped of high-grade sources of energy and other natural resources, and that these activities may be approaching the "limits of the earth" seem to affect public moods and attitudes scarcely at all.[4] Warnings of these hazards simply are not widely believed—yet. In such an intellectual-emotional milieu, it is to be expected that nearly all elected politicians will be reluctant to sponsor or support legislation that can be construed as a threat to this sanctified American dream. It seems apparent that it will take a good deal besides verbal admonitions to discredit expectations nourished from earliest childhood.

Expectations of more and more, indefinitely, acquire additional political significance from two concurrent trends: one is spreading politicization; the other, growing leverage by those capable of disrupting essential services.

There was a time when most of those who actually performed

the nitty-gritty services constituted the invisible poor. They were politically if not literally invisible in the sense that they had few or no effective channels of access to public authority. They were exploited and intimidated by their employers and ignored by their political representatives. Judges who administered the laws denied effective protection against hazards to which the poor were daily exposed in their grim struggle for survival. Their elementary needs could be, and were largely, ignored without risk of reprisal at the polls. They were, in effect, noncitizens in the national polity of which most of them were legally full-fledged members.

Some are still ignored, but their number is diminishing. Those who speak for the performers of essential services can make their demands heard, and those demands are likely to be heeded. This political muscle derives from numerous sources. To some extent it is attributable to the growth of unions.[5] But the new power can be attributed in greater degree to the dependence of our industrial-urban society upon uninterrupted delivery of a multitude of services.

Moreover, as previously emphasized, this latter source of vulnerability is amplified by concurrent increase of opportunities for illicit interventions and by the proneness of complex systems to break down from human failures and technical malfunctions. Vulnerabilities from these sources, and from accompanying community erosion, contribute to the statesmen's dilemma in various ways. Special significance arises from the increasing costs of repairing or preventing disrupted services, whether by eradicating underlying social causes or merely by shoring up the social order with more police and security apparatus. In either case, the result is additional and larger claims on insufficient disposable resources; and these rising costs directly or indirectly affect other allocations, including those for maintaining a reasonably safe and healthful physical habitat.

Another, often underrated, source of the statesmen's dilemma is the tightening interdependence of the inchoate world community. Chapter 6 emphasized the variety of transnational sources of vulnerability. These include much besides environmentally related military and military-associated hazards.[6] Special attention was given to the environmental implications of Third World demands for a larger share of the income and wealth to which the LDCs have contributed in energy and raw materials without (in their view) a fair return in industrial goods and services.

The extent to which the LDCs can and will pursue this objective can only be surmised. But as the oil embargo of 1973–1974 forewarned, even limited success in an essential economic sector can produce confusion and other adverse impacts on the economies of major consumers of energy and materials.

Still another source of the budgetary dilemma is the rising demand for more public money to aid municipalities to modernize antiquated sewerage systems, to sanitize trash disposal, to induce private industries to cease polluting air and water, and so forth. As evidence of damage and hazards to public health have received more publicity, and as the consequences have become more widely appreciated, demands for such programs have increased—and seem likely to increase indefinitely.

It is quite true that in the mid-1970s public attention shifted temporarily from pollutions to depletions. There are some indications that interested self-serving parties did all they could to promote this shift. It is also quite possible that alarmist rhetoric, designed to shake complacent citizens out of apathy and inertia, has fostered a credibility gap of skepticism. However, contrary to numerous predictions, demands for a safer, cleaner, quieter, more healthful milieu have not faded away. Scientific journals, newspapers, and other media continue to report and editorialize upon environmental news.

One indicator of the political impact of this persistent publicity, in legislative bodies, executive agencies, and the public prints and television, is gradually toughening enforcement of somewhat higher standards despite periodic setbacks, stubborn foot-dragging, drawn-out lawsuits, and some open defiance of the laws. Another indicator is the slowly expanding allocations of public as well as private funds for environmental protection.

Since the fuel shortages of 1973–1974 and 1976–1977, at least a few more citizens have begun to comprehend that spoliation of their country presents many problems, but also a single, multifaceted crisis of interrelated depletions, pollutions, and ecological disruptions.

An especially baffling feature of the statesmen's dilemma is the inexorably rising cost of dealing simultaneously with environmentally linked damage and hazards *and* with a multiplicity of vulnerabilities from other sources. This concurrence, we repeat, is the core of the dilemma of rising demands and insufficient disposable resources. It comes to a focus in the competition for public funds at every level of government, and it indirectly affects the expenditures of private industries and of individuals.

The dilemma is exacerbated by the inflexibility that is a chronic disease of all governmental financing. This inflexibility derives from several conditions. One is advance commitment of revenues to continuing projects. According to various calculations, no more than 10 to 15 percent of current federal, state, and local revenues are available for introduction or extension of programs of aid to education, basic and applied research, vocational retraining, renovation of public transportation, subsidies for low-income housing, support of public health services, infant day-care for working mothers, nonmilitary international relations, in addition to larger allocations for environmental repair and protection. In other words, all but a very small proportion of public revenues are preempted by contracts and other commitments that mortgage future revenues, in some instances for a decade or more in advance.[7]

Finally, governmental institutions and procedures at every level exhibit rigidities that intensify the statesmen's dilemma. Increasingly, professional students of government are investigating these rigidities in the specific context of environmental legislation, administration, litigation, and constituency relations.[8] As indicated in the Prologue, we recognize the importance of institutional constraints, even though we can consider them only briefly in this panoramic reconnaissance of the landscape of environmental politics.

Figure 1 categorizes the principal ingredients of the dilemma

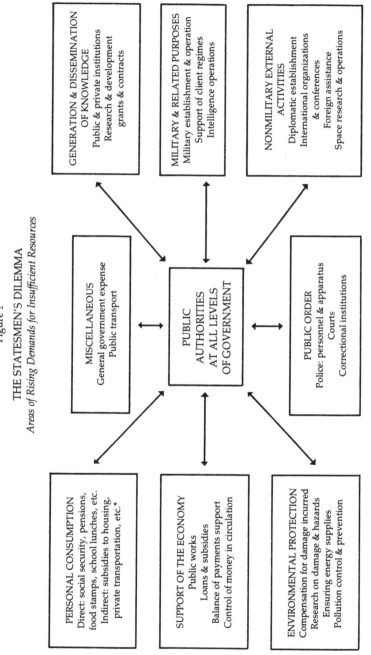

Figure 1

THE STATESMEN'S DILEMMA

Areas of Rising Demands for Insufficient Resources

GENERATION & DISSEMINATION OF KNOWLEDGE
Public & private institutions
Research & development grants & contracts

MILITARY & RELATED PURPOSES
Military establishment & operation
Support of client regimes
Intelligence operations

NONMILITARY EXTERNAL ACTIVITIES
Diplomatic establishment
International organizations & conferences
Foreign assistance
Space research & operations

MISCELLANEOUS
General government expense
Public transport

PUBLIC AUTHORITIES AT ALL LEVELS OF GOVERNMENT

PUBLIC ORDER
Police: personnel & apparatus
Courts
Correctional institutions

PERSONAL CONSUMPTION
Direct: social security, pensions, food stamps, school lunches, etc.
Indirect: subsidies to housing, private transportation, etc.*

SUPPORT OF THE ECONOMY
Public works
Loans & subsidies
Balance of payments support
Control of money in circulation

ENVIRONMENTAL PROTECTION
Compensation for damage incurred
Research on damage & hazards
Ensuring energy supplies
Pollution control & prevention

*Categories of competing demands here and below are suggestive, but not necessarily comprehensive.

of proliferating and rising demands on grossly insufficient disposable resources. The double-headed arrows emphasize the two-way relationship of claims and responses. Furthermore, when interpreting the figure one should remember that responses include not only direct allocations of funds from tax returns and other public funds, but also allocations through private channels that are significantly affected by such governmental policies as the amount of currency in circulation, incidence of taxation, interest rates, and other indirect methods of affecting distribution and uses of the national product.

For instance, in the category of "personal consumption," some of the goods and services are derived from old-age pensions and other annuities from public funds, welfare grants, and the like. However, in the United States, a large part of personal consumption derives from nongovernmental sources, such as salaries and wages from private employment, profits from business, interest on nongovernmental investments, privately financed pensions, and so on. Even these are indirectly affected by governmental policies, as exemplified in personal and corporate income taxes, real estate taxes, and flat-rate sales taxes that not only provide funds for governmental operations but also affect the distribution of spendable income in private hands.

This duality is evident in other categories: in the mixture of public and private investments in fixed capital, in support of education and research, in contributions to reductions of pollutions, and numerous other operations. In short, nearly everywhere the hand of public authority is increasingly evident, allocating funds directly, or influencing their allocation indirectly in the private sector.

Figure 1 offers no specific data or solutions. Its function is rather to direct attention to some of the conditions that put the statesmen's dilemma at the core of environmental politics. Rearranging the categories of the figure brings the centrality of environmental costs into still sharper focus. As described in chapter 5, expanding industrial development and accompanying urbanization have proliferated and increased the costs of maintaining a functionally durable society and a reasonably stable physical habitat. Despite a steady barrage of demands for less government, rising expenditures and taxes reflect an expanding rather than a shrinking role of public authority in support of the military services, human resources, and environmental repair and protection. Concurrent peaking of claims and commitments in these three major categories and in others designated in Figure 1, along with increasing insufficiency of disposable funds, is another way of defining the statesmen's dilemma.

Priorities and Resources: Patterns and Trends

Before considering various approaches to this dilemma, let us examine some comparative data on governmental expenditures during recent years. Figure 2 compares federal expenditures by categories since 1961, in dollars of current value from year to year. Figure 3 compares these allocations as fractions of total federal expenditures, also in current dollars. Figure 4 compares allocations as fractions of the GNP.[9]

Much of the discussion of budgetary priorities has focused on trends in allocations for military and military-related purposes. On this issue one discovers apparently irreconcilable disagreement. Nearly a generation ago, General Eisenhower, recently inaugurated as president, anticipated one side of a confrontation that continues to this day. He said: "Every gun that is made, every warship launched, every rocket fired signifies, in the final sense, a theft from those who hunger and are not fed, those who are cold and are not clothed. This world in arms is not spending money alone. It is spending the sweat of its laborers, the genius of its scientists, the hopes of its children."[10]

Some years later, economist Robert Heilbroner declared the military budget to be a "disaster for America. It has sucked into the service of fear and death the energies and resources desperately needed for hope and life."[11]

Advocates of higher military budgets usually make their case

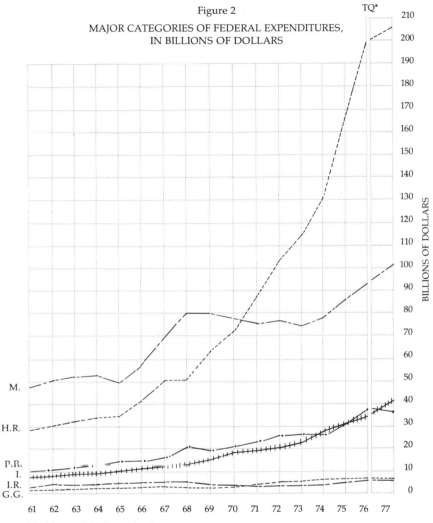

Figure 2

MAJOR CATEGORIES OF FEDERAL EXPENDITURES, IN BILLIONS OF DOLLARS

M. –Military & Military-related
H.R. –Human Resources: education & manpower, health, income security, veterans' benefits & services
P.R. –Physical Resources: agriculture, natural resources & environment, commerce & transportation, community development & housing
I. –Interest on national debt
I.R. –Nonmilitary International Relations
G.G. –General Government

Source: Data from *United States Budget in Brief, Fiscal Year 1971* and *Fiscal Year 1977*.

*Transition quarter, July 1–Sept. 30, 1976, resulted when beginning of fiscal year was shifted from July 1 to Oct. 1.

Figure 3

MAJOR CATEGORIES OF FEDERAL EXPENDITURES, AS PERCENTAGES OF TOTAL FEDERAL EXPENDITURES

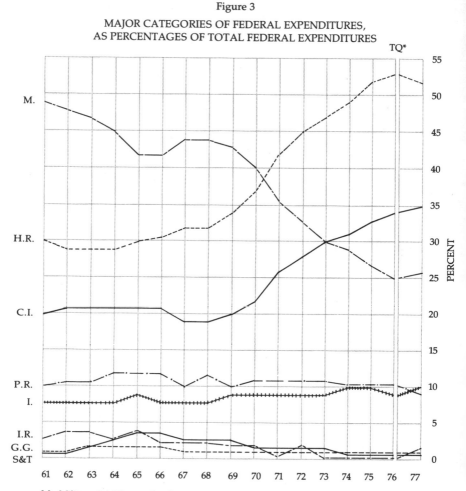

M.–Military & Military-related
H.R.–Human Resources: education & manpower, health, income security, veterans' benefits & services
C.I.–Civilian Income, abstracted from Human Resources
P.R.–Physical Resources: agriculture, natural resources & environment, commerce & transportation, community development & housing
I.–Interest on national debt
I.R.–Nonmilitary International Relations
G.G.–General Government
S&T–Space & Technology

Source: Data from *United States Budget in Brief, Fiscal Year 1971* and *Fiscal Year 1977*.

*Transition quarter, July 1–Sept. 30, 1976, resulted when beginning of fiscal year was shifted from July 1 to Oct. 1.

Figure 4

MAJOR CATEGORIES OF FEDERAL EXPENDITURES, AS PERCENTAGES OF GROSS NATIONAL PRODUCT

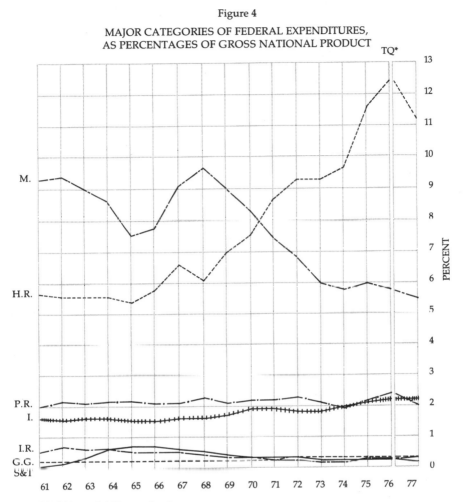

M.–Military & Military-related
H.R.–Human Resources: education & manpower, health, income security, veterans' benefits & services
P.R.–Physical Resources: agriculture, natural resources & environment, commerce & transportation, community development & housing
I.–Interest on national debt
I.R.–Nonmilitary International Relations
G.G.–General Government
S&T–Space & Technology

Source: Data from *United States Budget in Brief, Fiscal Year 1971* and *Fiscal Year 1977*.

*Transition quarter, July 1–Sept. 30, 1976, resulted when beginning of fiscal year was shifted from July 1 to Oct. 1.

with little or no apparent concern for societal and environmental vulnerabilities. A fair sample is a statement by M. T. Yarymovych (who identified himself, in 1973, as "chief scientist for the U.S. Air Force"). He contended that the high level of military expenditures had prevented a nuclear war for 28 years (that is, as of 1973); that the military establishment had been receiving a progressively smaller share of the national product as well as a smaller percentage of federal appropriations; and that post-Vietnam reorganization and renovation of the military services would require more money than it had been getting.[12]

This debate heats up every year during the period of federal budget making. Neither side has a monopoly of truth or wisdom. Each can and does cite some hard evidence, but also much soft speculation. The contradictory conclusions reflect profoundly different conceptions of what vulnerabilities are more threatening, and what claims should take precedence.

Advocates of larger military budgets rest their case on the most pessimistic assumptions about American-Soviet relations and the risk of a surprise attack on the United States. They make extremely optimistic assumptions regarding realizable American economic capabilities, present and future, and regarding putative benefits derivable from competitive militarism.

Those who attack the high level of military spending base their case on less optimistic assumptions regarding the deterrent value of technological militarism. They also pay more attention to the multiplicity and severity of nonmilitary hazards both domestic and transnational, and to the gross insufficiency of federal revenues to cover these hazards and at the same time play out the risky game of competitive militarism. We shall return to this issue in the Epilogue, in the light of data exhibited in Figures 2–4.[13]

Inspection of these three figures reveals that military and military-related allocations, though large and currently expanding (in current dollars), actually command a less favored position than formerly. As indicated in Figure 2, military expenditures in 1961 totaled approximately $47 billions. By 1972 this allocation had risen to nearly $78 billions. As of late 1976, the official estimate for 1977 exceeded $100 billions (still in current dollars with no adjustment for inflation).[14]

Assuming total military allocations by the end of fiscal 1978 to be $110 billions, or even more, these may still reflect some shrinkage in actual purchasing power—that is, in dollars of constant value, calculated from some previous year. Furthermore, viewed in relation to *all* federal expenditures (Figure 3), the allocation to military purposes declined from approximately 48 percent in 1961 to about 32 percent in 1972, to an estimated 25 percent in 1977. Numerous presently conjectural variables will determine how far this trend will continue during America's third century.

The recent downward trend in the military's share of federal revenues during the 1970s runs counter to the trend in a composite "human resources" category. This composite includes social security payments, civil service (but not military) pensions, federal contributions to education, health services, veterans' benefits, support of the destitute, and a few lesser items. Latest available estimates at this writing for the category have risen (in current dollars) from about $29 billions in 1961 to more than $200 billions. Thus, while military expenditures declined from 48 to 25 percent of all federal expenditures, those for support of human resources during the same period rose from about 30 percent to over 50 percent.

As fractions of the GNP, the corresponding percentage changes were: human resources increased from 5.5 percent in 1961 to over 12; military decreased from a bit over 9 (a level reached three times during the 1960s) to about 6. That is, we are now approaching the end of the second consecutive decade in which military budgets have risen in current dollars but declined as a fraction of total federal expenditures and as a fraction of the GNP, while allocations for human resources have risen more than those for the military have fallen—differential trends exhibited in Figures 3 and 4.

Comparing federal military and human-resources allocations

with those for repair and protection of the physical habitat presents greater difficulty. This arises in part because federal budgeteers have failed to define a stable category that includes all or even most environmental expenditures. Hence it is still impossible to determine very precisely how much the federal government was actually allocating to this cluster of functions in the 1960s and early 1970s, or how much it is allocating today.

The first report of the Council on Environmental Quality estimated federal funding for "pollution and abatement" at $763 millions in 1969 and at $885 millions in 1970, and predicted it would be $1.38 billions for 1971.[15]

For the same three years, the *U.S. Budget in Brief* subsumed environmental costs under the category of "natural resources." Outlays in this category were reported to have been slightly more than $2 billions in fiscal 1969, $2.5 billions in 1970, and $2.7 billions in 1971.[16]

Several years later, this category (which in 1973 had been relabeled "natural resources and environment") was expanded retrospectively to include "energy," and the outlays were revised upward to nearly $4 billions for 1969, $4 billions for 1970, and $4.9 billions for 1972. As of late 1976, the estimate for 1977 (manifestly subject to further revision) was $13.8 billions. Just before retiring as administrator of EPA in January 1977, Russell Train complained that the staff and funds allocated to his agency were still grossly inadequate to perform the services specified by law.[17]

Taking the highest revised total for 1970, the allocation for "natural resources, environment, and energy" was about 5 percent of military, and 5.5 percent of human resources expenditures. In the provisional estimate for 1977 the levels were 13.6 and 6.7 percent respectively. Still using the highest 1970 statistic, environmentally related expenditures were then about 1.4 percent of GNP, and were estimated at less than 1 percent for 1977.[18]

Adding in state and local budgets changes the proportions somewhat. Military defense is almost exclusively a federally

financed function. Hence its share of total governmental allocations at *all* levels would seem to be somewhat lower than the
above percentages indicate. On the other hand, state and local
budgets are heavily weighted with costs of education, welfare,
waste disposal, and other human-resources and environmental
items—functions only partially financed by federal loans or
grants. This fact gives these nonmilitary categories somewhat
higher percentages of total public expenditures. However, the
addition of state and local contributions does not evade or resolve the statesmen's dilemma of grossly insufficient disposable
resources to cope with the multiplying vulnerabilities from diverse sources to which Americans are exposed.

The federal budgetary category of "international affairs and
finance" includes—in addition to support of the Department of
State, the Foreign Service, the United Nations, and other international agencies—most of the nonmilitary technical and material assistance given to LDCs from federal funds. Every president
since World War II has declared such assistance to be a vital
concern of the United States. Yet never in recent years have
allocations for nonmilitary international relations ever taken as
much as 5 percent of federal funds. The combined outlays for
all such functions have never in the 1970s run as high as 4 percent; in 1976 they accounted for only 1.5 percent. This is about
6 percent of the allocation for military and military-related purposes—a stark exhibit of the extremely low priority which our
chosen rulers assign to diplomacy, international organization,
sharing of intellectual and material resources with less affluent
units of the world community—and participating in international programs to arrest accelerative deterioration of the global
physical habitat, to which many of our more refractory domestic
problems are related.

Any substantial increase in aid to the LDCs will have to come
from larger resources at the disposal of federal agencies or from
changes in current priorities. Either alternative, or the effort to
maintain the status quo, seems likely to react on the prices paid
for fuel and other essential imports, on the distribution of in-

come within the United States, and on taxation and perhaps other policies at all levels of government. The urgency of these transnational nonmilitary allocations is endlessly disputed.

The statesmen's dilemma is extended and tightened if numerous lesser allocations are taken into consideration: among others, interest on public debts and miscellaneous costs of governmental administration. However, from the standpoint of environmental repair and protection, the budgetary components of greater immediate significance are the allocations for military and military-related and human-resources support. These together consume over three-quarters of all federal revenues; and the latter takes a large share of public expenditures at state and local levels also. Partly for this reason, we shall concentrate in the rest of this chapter mainly on the fiscal interrelations of the military, human-resources, and environmental budgets.

Since about 1960 much of the discussion of social and environmental needs has tacitly assumed the priority of military demands and commitments. Frequently allocations for these purposes have been discussed as if the military establishment and military-related operations were financed from some mysterious "surplus" of dollars unavailable for the needs of the domestic society and its physical habitat. When such notions are overtly challenged, as they have been within the last few years, and when the challengers openly defy the mystique of chauvinistic nationalism and the hubris of a self-appointed global mission, then social and environmental needs begin to compete with military demands on slightly less unfavorable terms.

Numerous writers have demonstrated statistically how much even minor changes in budgetary priorities might accomplish. Such comparisons emphasize the social and environmental cost-equivalents of military hardware, manned sorties into outer space, superhighway programs, and other projects that have received tens or scores of billions of dollars in public revenues during the past generation.[19]

There is no certainty, of course, that some prudential pruning of military and other appropriations, and tighter accounting for military expenditures in particular, would yield larger allocations for social and environmental purposes. Congress and state legislatures might opt instead for reduction of taxes—a course that one can confidently predict would be applauded on every Main Street in America.

Be that as it may, debates on appropriations for the military services and their industrial allies, for military research and development, for so-called client regimes, and for other military-related purposes are no longer conducted without reference to our societal malaise, deteriorating habitat, and other nonmilitary vulnerabilities. From the later 1960s, congressional and other defenders of the military budget have found it increasingly necessary to justify their demands within the context of ethical and material impacts on the domestic society and its physical habitat. What seems to be happening is a progressive mergence of traditionally more or less mutually isolated military and nonmilitary, foreign and domestic, national and local issues into a single indivisible politics of the American national community as a whole.

This mergence has been deplored by a few observers. Among these are the residual advocates of a "pax Americana." One of these has acknowledged that "the United States cannot effectively implement global primacy . . . unless it manages to insulate its society and economy from traumatic impacts by each and every peripheral military involvement."[20]

The author of that lament was speaking with special reference to the then escalating Vietnam war, which evoked rising opposition within the United States. One might query whether that protracted war—with 50,000 Americans killed and hundreds of thousands injured—was a "peripheral military involvement." However, such understatements do not diminish the cogency of the argument that progressive mergence of internal and external politics significantly affects the ordering of national priorities, including many if not all of the problems arising in the social and physical environments.

An analogous interplay of competing priorities has accompanied the allocations of billions for the research and hardware necessary for manned sorties into outer space. For example, an editorial in the *Bulletin of the Atomic Scientists* several years ago lamented that funds for space projects were likely to be curtailed in order to provide more for alleviation of hunger and want within the United States. The author of that lament predicted that "the future of manned space flight depends on whether it is possible to separate space exploration as an investment in the future from the immediate demands of socioeconomic problems."[21]

Others have translated this jargon into plainer English: whether space exploration should take precedence over letting the poor and destitute go hungry; whether ghettolike slums should be tolerated; whether the elderly should be neglected— in short, whether putting a few astronauts upon the moon, or wherever in outer space, should take priority over a lengthening agenda of overdue social reforms, at least some of which may have significant bearing not only on the state of the physical habitat but also on the future of the American national community right here upon the earth.

Some social activists are prone to pit "human" needs against environmental programs. This is not so difficult to do, partly because (whatever the merits) the latter have become more or less identified in certain quarters with the higher-income classes. Environmental repair and protection, such activists contend, should remain in the refrigerator until more "urgent" human needs are met in behalf of the poor and destitute—needs for better food, housing, education, child-care, health services, and the like. From this viewpoint, ecology is perceived as a subtle plot for prettifying the playgrounds of the affluent at the price of perpetuating the miseries of the poor.

Some politicians have given subtle, and not so subtle, support to this image. Consider, for example, a statement made by a former chairman of the Democratic National Committee. He gave lip service to the need for cleaner air and water, and to the hazard of pesticides that are "upsetting the balance of Nature." He likewise acknowledged that "in the long run, unless we get a handle on these problems, mankind may be doomed." But where in the scale of current priorities, he asked, "is air pollution in the mind of a mother in the core city whose baby has been bitten by a rat? What priority does a polluted lake have to a family whose main recreation area is a littered alley? . . . What priority do open spaces occupy in the minds of thousands . . . who are born, exist, and die in congested, dangerous slums?"[22]

That politician did not exaggerate the indignities and privations inflicted on the poor and destitute. Nor did he ignore the importance of getting on with the macro-problems of environmental protection. But he did omit some decidedly relevant variables. He said not one word about the military budget that was then preempting 35 percent of all federal revenue, and nearly 7 percent of the GNP, much of it spent on destroying the people and their habitat in Vietnam and adjacent countries. He said nothing about the concealed subsidies to the private trucking industry implicit in the national superhighway program. He said nothing about the billions allocated to beating the Russians to the moon. These omissions were not unique or eccentric. They were simply typical exhibits of the compartmented thinking that continues to be prevalent among politicians, bureaucrats, many academic scholars, and a great many others who have habitually isolated allocations for certain purposes from social and environmental imperatives.

The late Whitney Young (director of the Urban League) was probably correct when he accused some "environmental crusaders" of finding their cause a welcome diversion from the ubiquitous issues of poverty, discrimination, and privilege. But he too ignored the outlays for the military services, for superhighways, and for explorations of outer space. He too failed to recognize, or at least to acknowledge, that slum dwellers need *all* the essentials of a reasonably healthful and safe environment. Indeed, by our lights, they need these elemental essentials where they are forced to live, work, and play, even more than their more affluent fellow citizens who retire to the suburbs daily, and periodically escape for extended vacations, away from chronic grey overcast, recurrent smog, incessant noise, and the filth and other pollutions of our industrial towns and cities.[23]

From this perspective, the choice is not an either/or one of attending to poverty and discrimination or neglecting these to attend to pollution of the physical habitat. Obviously the need is to attend to both, and for much the same reasons. Both are ingredients of a single problem, the problem of keeping America decently livable, and of doing this in such a way as to minimize as much as possible the gross inequalities that still permeate American society.

For this reason, if for no other, social and environmental activists might profitably examine the advantages of an alliance of convenience if not of conviction. That is, they might both become politically more effective if they could make common cause against glut, waste, and the current ordering of priorities, while pressing their respective claims for larger shares of the resources at the disposal of public authorities.

The alternative—mutual recrimination and hostile confrontation—simply pits environmental and other human needs against each other, with resultant injury to both causes. Specifically, any program for spending large sums for cleaner air and the rest of the items on the agenda of environmental reform runs into grave political trouble if these values are pushed ahead of more adequate outlays to eradicate poverty and the conditions and consequences of poverty—and vice versa.[24]

Summing up: environmental politics evokes questions regarding who gets what, who pays, and who will suffer in consequence. As soon as one crosses the fiscal threshold of budgetary priorities, he runs into questions regarding impacts on military demands, on exploration of outer space, on nonmilitary international relations, on social melioration of all kinds, on highway building, on public transportation, on incidence and levels of taxation, on personal expectations, and on still other facets of the ongoing economic-social-political order.

It is politically impossible to dissociate environmental repair and protection from the gross inadequacy of disposable dollars to cope with this much larger congeries of vulnerabilities and other claims from diverse sources. In the mélange of multiple competing claims, and the inevitable interactions of competitive claimants for these insufficient disposable resources, we see a prime exhibit of the interrelatedness that is ipso facto an invariable element of the context of environmental politics.

~(9)~

Unfinished Business
The Setting

THE WORLD OF 2000, less than 25 years hence, may differ from today's as much as the present differs from 1900. One might also speculate that the world of 2076, if our republic survives to the end of its third century, would seem as strange to the celebrants of 1976 as the present would have seemed to the thousands who journeyed to the Philadelphia Centennial Exposition in 1876. Americans (along with the rest of humankind) are living in an era of radical transition. Physical and cultural landscapes are changing at rates previously unknown; and some of these changes are proliferating hazards likewise unknown in "the world we have lost."[1]

The dimensions of these newer hazards are much in dispute. Suggestions that the physical and social environments are becoming in important respects less safe and healthful, and less supportive of human dignity and freedom as well as of material well-being, have evoked vigorous dissents. The common denominator of these is that science-based industrialism enables more people to enjoy more material amenities and more leisure than ever in the past.

In stressing the vulnerabilities that proliferate with many advances in applied science, we do not minimize hazards to which people have been and still are exposed in earlier stages of this progression. Severely limited power over the physical environment persisted everywhere well into the present century. Millions of Americans still living in the 1970s remember a world in which no one enjoyed security against a multiplicity of hazards from which nearly all but the very poor and destitute have more or less escaped today. However, in the course of this material progress, new conditions have emerged that expose all humans to hazards more lasting than those confronted in the America of 1900. Consider a few examples, all of which have been cited in previous chapters.

First, the enormous advance in the technology of killing people and destroying their habitat: Existing stockpiles of late-model superweapons represent a capability not only to kill on a scale without precedent but also to render large regions, possibly the entire earth, uninhabitable. What pre-1945 hazard presented a comparable threat to whole nations and their living space?

Second, the rapidly expanding grid of nuclear-fission power plants: The mining, processing, and burning of fossil fuels have always presented serious risks, but those risks are trivial compared with hazards inherent in an emerging worldwide weapons-linked, nuclear-fission power industry and a related global traffic in nuclear technology. Large-scale accidental or malevolent release into the environment of radioactive poisons poses hazards far beyond the life-span of those who optimistically play down this source of long-enduring disasters.

Third, a mélange of hazards from exposure to more or less harmful as well as definitely lethal synthetic products and residues of expanding chemical industries: Such materials are reported to number thousands of different items, with new ones entering the environment every year. These include pesticides, herbicides, food additives, medical drugs, industrial reagents and residues, and many others. Furthermore, in many instances their malign effects on human health as well as on property are not immediately determinable. Their potential for damage may not emerge conclusively until decades after exposure; and by then the damage, or much of it, may have become irreparable.

Fourth, the widening imbalance between worldwide population increase and food production: This imbalance is not a new phenomenon. What is relatively new is the magnitude of the hazard. Damage from this source can extend beyond a single generation. It threatens to tighten a vicious circle which makes difficult, if it does not totally preclude, escape from the hazard of future generations mentally incapable of coping with the complexities of an increasingly crowded earth.

Fifth, hazards latent in current research agendas in biochemistry: It is now becoming possible to create new species by recombining the genes of existing species of microbes and larger organisms. This emergent capability may produce new approaches to presently incurable diseases. It may even open the door to expanded food production and produce still other benefits, as advocates of "genetic engineering" confidently anticipate. However, recombining genes may also produce incalculable damage as previously suggested, possibly including sooner or later a capability (it is hinted) to create humanlike robots or more sinister monsters.

Never, prior to the 1940s, was the human population exposed to hazards of man-made origin that could render great cities, entire countries, larger regions, even possibly the entire earth unfit for human habitation. In this respect, historic hazards were not in the same ball park, not even in the same league, with some of those existent or in prospect today. For this reason, if for no other, it seems to us irrelevant, deceptive, and socially irresponsible to minimize today's and tomorrow's unprecedented hazards by comparing them with those of the past.

It is likewise misleading to minimize the risk of damage that could persist indefinitely, by comparing such hazards with the risk of death by automobile or aircraft, or by collapse of dams or other defective products of contemporary engineering. Such comparisons seem to us about as credible as predicting the weather of the year 2076 by simple extrapolation from the weather records of 1976.

Cumulative piecemeal erosion of the biosphere, as repeatedly emphasized, also presents hazards not only formidable but also subtle and insidious. It has been a piecemeal process because much of the damage has not arisen from spectacular events, comparable to explosion of the first atomic bomb, but rather from innumerable small happenings. It has been subtle because (with infrequent exceptions) environmentally destructive events have usually attracted relatively little public attention at the time of occurrence. It has been insidious because the cumulative deterioration of the habitat has generally gone unnoticed—except by a few environmental scientists and amateur naturalists—until major damage has resulted. The process is somewhat analogous to the scarcely discernible advance of a glacier until it is suddenly perceived to be engulfing a whole valley.

What should be done? This and related questions have evoked endless discussion but no consensus. To paraphrase (and mangle) an overworked but still useful metaphor: All humans— rich and poor, young and old, learned and ignorant, altruistic and self-serving—are crowded into an increasingly overloaded spacecraft, threatened with dwindling food, fuel, and other essentials, and navigated by officers equipped with obsolescent charts and limited relevant knowledge. Manifestly, the consequent uncertainties, perplexities, frustrations, and anxieties make for a quarrelsome voyage, rife with disputations regarding destination, course, portents, and hazards.

Here is a state of affairs to inspire futuristic speculation; and that is one commodity of which there is no current shortage. To the extent that sorties into futurism influence public thinking and penetrate the minds of public authorities, and thereby affect governmental policies and business practices, they become ingredients of the context of environmental politics. Some of these futuristic scenarios have been examined in previous chapters; but those and a few others deserve a little further attention before we sign off.

Most pervasive of all seems to be the image that disorders attributed to depletions of fossil fuels and other natural resources, and to resultant pollutions and ecological disruptions, are unlikely to be serious impediments to economic growth and the spread of industrial society. Such expectations are buttressed by public assurances of eminent scientists, economists and business leaders, who assert that technological innovation and the marketplace, with minimal governmental interference, can surmount all obstacles that may arise; and that continued economic growth can supply the goods and services necessary to support simultaneously competitive militarism, further sorties into outer space, the amenities of middle- and upper-class living, handouts to the poor and destitute—and concurrently cope with energy shortages, pollutions, and other deteriorations of the physical habitat.[2]

As for the next decade, or perhaps the rest of the twentieth century, this scenario does not seem to us necessarily incredible. But in the longer stretch of America's third century as a whole, it raises doubts and queries, some of which we have already recorded in chapters 3 and 8, and elsewhere.

At the other end of the spectrum, one finds numerous scenarios that envisage some kind of irretrievable catastrophe as the most likely culmination of current policies and trends.

Most dramatic are the predictions of doomsday by thermonuclear war. These are based in part upon the well-established fragility of contemporary industrial societies, and in part upon optimistic assumptions regarding the hazards of lethal radioactive fallout. Authors of these scenarios disagree about the consequences of such a catastrophe. But there seems to be relatively little dissent from the expectation that large-scale use of such weapons would reduce any surviving remnant of humankind to a primitive existence in a scorched and genetically precarious habitat. What is envisioned is a stunning climax with indefinitely irreparable destruction of the essential features of contemporary industrial society, and at worst the total destruction of life and the habitat that sustains it.[3]

Another line of apocalyptic conjecture envisions accelerative pollution and disruption of the biosphere, which would reduce its habitability to zero. At least one version of this scenario projects zero-habitability within a few decades. Others envisage a comparable outcome through a longer time span, to result from the continuing exploitive practices of current industrial systems and the still-unmanageable global increase of population.[4]

A less apocalyptic scenario at the pessimistic end of the spectrum is the "limits to growth" model, and its sequel, the study entitled *Mankind at the Turning Point*, both sponsored by the Club of Rome. The former, which we examined in some detail in chapter 2, projects a rather abrupt collapse of industrial society within a century or so *if* certain specified dysfunctional trends are allowed to continue.[5]

These pessimistic scenarios, to which others could be added, are not science fiction. Nor are they absurd maunderings of ignorant or disordered minds, as numerous physical scientists and economists seem to believe. They present sober, well-informed calculations by highly qualified and widely respected scientists and other professionals in several relevant specialties. Their futuristic conjectures are just as likely, in our judgment, to prove correct as the optimistic and hubristic predictions of numerous economists and physical scientists.

It should be emphasized that the samples cited above do not project inevitable "doom," as some critics have mistakenly charged. All hold out hope, explicitly or implicitly, that terminal catastrophe can be avoided if certain essential changes in institutions, policies, and practices are introduced in time. However, at least some of the more pessimistic futurists indulge in rhetoric that seems to imply doubt that such policy changes will actually occur, at least within the framework of relatively open societies.

Numerous futuristic scenarios include policy prescriptions. One example claims that only authoritarian rule can cope with an advanced state of environmental disruption. The author of that scenario resurrects the political philosophies of Plato, Hobbes, and other historic skeptics of democratic government. The argument is that only enlightened and benevolent dictators can impose and enforce the harsh restrictions that will be necessary to arrest the ruinous drift toward environmental ruin.[6] We recognize the problem, but we do not share the expectation that authoritarian rule would be either environmentally enlightened or humanely benevolent. On the contrary, it seems to us a prescription for combining power with irresponsibility, a recipe that has repeatedly produced unenlightened and inhumane despotism.

Other prescriptions envision rescue by putting scientists and engineers in the driver's seat—in short, what is usually called technocracy. In one version only pure and applied science can provide the knowledge, tools, and know-how necessary to sustain life on a denuded and progressively polluted earth. Another version envisions permanent self-sustaining colonies in outer space to which some remnant of humankind can migrate and survive if the earth becomes unfit for habitation.

Technocratic prescriptions seem to us as unpromising as resort to "philosopher-kings." We have repeatedly emphasized our conviction of the essential role of creative scientists and innovative engineers—but as contributors to a complex political process, not as determiners of environmental policies and the social order.

We have recorded our objections to Weinberg's "Faustian bargain" for propping up the status quo through a few more decades by massive infusions of energy from fission-powered reactors fueled chiefly with plutonium, the most lethal substance yet produced by nuclear scientists. That too seems to us to entail grave unresolved hazards and erosion of civil rights as the price of a problematical reprieve for current-style industrial society.

Research and experiments in recombinant DNA evoke comparable misgivings. These too entail as yet undetermined hazards. Many in our society, including some eminent biochemists, regard this agenda as a Pandora's box too dangerous to open any farther until more is learned about latent hazards and the possibility of containing them.

We have taken notice of the apparently spreading vogue of the so-called lifeboat ethic, to be implemented by a "triage strategy." (Triage is a military expression denoting the practice in World War II of dividing the wounded into three categories: those who would survive without immediate medical attention; those who would presumably recover if they received prompt medical attention; and those who would probably die regardless of care.)

This strategy has been resurrected in various contexts as an approach to the intractable imbalance between population increase and accessible food in hunger-ridden regions. The scheme envisions American public authorities, relatively secure in their currently well-provisioned first-class lifeboat, serving their constituencies by ignoring the pleas of starving peoples judged by the affluent to be "unsalvageable."[7]

This proposal is a logical heir of the hoary principle that food and nearly everything else should be distributed internationally as well as domestically in accord with ability to pay. The latter principle seems likely to promote, as well as condone, reduction of population by starvation and associated diseases in many of the poorer countries as surely as does the triage strategy defended by the lifeboat ethic.

All futuristic scenarios embody elements of uncertainty that are sometimes obscured by dogmatic rhetoric. No one today can plausibly claim to *know* the world of 2000, much less the world of 2076. The intervening years will surely spring many surprises. In view of prospective advances in knowledge, especially in the natural sciences but also in the art of governance, it would seem naïve to anticipate that the next century, or even quarter-century, can be foreknown by linear extrapolation of the recent past. However, as many have emphasized, it is possible today to learn more about some of the conditions that may affect the future, even though all futuristic scenarios still embody a large ingredient of indeterminacy.

Possibly the greatest source of indeterminacy is the human response to a milieu that is changing at rates unknown in the past. Nearly all (including those who speak in pseudo-deterministic rhetoric) behave as if human choices do affect the future. At the same time, the range of effective choices—choices that can be successfully implemented—is not unlimited. There is plenty of disagreement about the sources and rigidity of limiting conditions. What actually happens may be contingent on changing wants and norms, changing boundaries of knowledge, changing tools and skills, and other cultural changes—or by changes in nonhuman nature or even by events in outer space.

Beyond such limitations there remains the question whether there are ultimate limits inherent in a habitat that, in a material sense, is a closed system except for inputs of solar energy.[8] On this question, we repeat, we can discover no approach to consensus. In general, environmental scientists seem to recognize and respect such limits to a greater extent than do most physicists and economists. It seems reasonable to us that the higher the rates of environmental depletions and pollutions, the narrower will become the range of effective choices and the more regimented will become the lives of individuals.[9]

Manifestly, nothing will be accomplished unless something is undertaken, though any undertaking may fall short of desired results if limiting conditions are either unknown or disregarded, or are beyond control. For example, a strategy to resolve the statesmen's dilemma by perpetually expanding economic output may be frustrated by obstacles, social or nonhuman, that limit the rate or duration of economic growth.

Some obstacles are wholly or partially external to the actors in a situation; among others, cumbersome legislative and administrative procedures, budgetary inflexibility resulting from advance commitments of revenues, multiplicity and diversity of claims on insufficient disposable revenues, limitations of knowledge and available equipment, and inaccessibility of sufficient energy and materials.

Additional obstacles may derive from the personalities and calculations of the policymakers—their biases, their limited understanding, their impressions of public tolerance, and the like. Nearly always, in the United States as in other relatively open societies, governmental decisions reflect intuitive impressions as to what and how much the political traffic will bear.

The record suggests that such impressions, however imprecise, are often determinative. The politicians' images of what is politically feasible may be naïve or sophisticated, or skewed by their own prejudices. However, there seems generally to be considerable congruence between widely prevailing public moods, attitudes, and tolerances, and official responses thereto. Hence, the importance we attach to public postures that inhibit more rapid progress toward a safer, cleaner, quieter, and more healthful habitat.

We are nearing the end of two decades of continuous publicity regarding dysfunctional changes in the life-supportive biosphere. Despite this exposure, millions remain apathetic, ill informed, and generally skeptical of environmental hazards that may adversely affect their own lives and expectations.

That is not to deny that more people have become aware of recurrent smog, grayish brown overcast, and other unpleasant qualities of the air they breathe. They are likewise more aware of the fouling of once relatively clean lakes, streams, and tidal waters. They may have learned something about the hazards of "sanitary landfills" that are far from sanitary. They may have paid some attention to landscapes eroded and otherwise damaged by agricultural and industrial processes. They have observed the creeping intrusions of concrete and asphalt. They are irritated by increasing noise, especially if they live around air ports and many types of industrial plants. A few have deplored the destruction of plant and animal species and their habitats, and still other evidence of a depreciating physical habitat.

However, there is remarkably little evidence that many Americans are even half-persuaded that these changes in their habitat pose serious threats to themselves or to their children and grandchildren. Environmental repair and protection seem to be rather generally regarded as a worthy cause, but at the same time as a luxury, more or less, for which someone else will pay. In any case, there seems to be a widely prevailing view that this cause is one that can safely remain upon the back burner until more urgent wants are assured, such as better and more secure jobs, larger business profits, longer vacations, and a lengthening list of other wants and amenities.

Our observation of this passive mood evokes some doubt about how much protective action can plausibly be anticipated until more people experience some jolts that raise their consciousness of a personal stake in a decently livable physical habitat. How much can be expected until many more citizens experience really severe privations? More chronic physical unfitness? More unpleasant reminders that America may have crossed a threshold from an era of expanding abundance to one of multiplying shortages and still more damaging pollutions?

As many have emphasized, most Americans have grown up to believe instead in a future of indefinitely expanding opportunities, less need for tedious hard work, greater quantities of worldly goods, and more leisure in which to enjoy them. So far as we can determine, the notion that these expectations may prove to be only seductive mirages is incredible, indeed almost unthinkable, to countless millions. Such a prospect is summarily dismissed as pernicious nonsense by most economists, businessmen, politicians, and citizens in general.

We observe a rather general propensity to shut one's eyes and ears as long as possible to frightening portents. Such has clearly been the more-or-less prevalent reaction to the continuing menace of nuclear war. Something similar seems to have occurred in response to warnings of environmental disasters. Most Americans seem to be much more concerned about debts and taxes, the escalating cost of education, even the wherewithal to live comfortably from month to month. In short, their chief concerns are with the here and now, not with warnings of future disasters about which they comprehend little, and which they do not really believe will occur. Such has been clearly the response to date to the energy shortfalls of 1973–1974 and 1976–1977.[10]

The American nation is the richest and by far the largest consumer of energy, but to date there have been only perfunctory gestures toward conservation. Americans seem to take for granted that they have an inalienable right to consume upwards of half of the world's marketed energy supplies. This profligacy prevails despite credible testimony from qualified experts that conservation, achieved by eliminating waste in industry, transport, and household use, could reduce consumption by 20 to 40 percent or more without significantly reducing business profits (with a few exceptions) or eroding the average personal standard of living.[11]

This record evokes further questions. How much attention is likely to be paid to warnings of dire hazards, if these are attacked only with weak incentives? If the issue were put to a vote, would *any* majority of Americans—well-to-do, middle income, or poor—opt to protect their posterity, or even their own safety and health five to ten years hence, if the anticipated price of doing so includes higher taxes, smaller cars, increasingly expensive energy costs, endlessly rising prices for food and housing, and other inroads of inflation on their accustomed style of living? A British reviewer of John Quarles's modest but relatively optimistic assessment of the EPA's achievements has tried to answer these questions. The reviewer acknowledged the hazards but queried the limits of American tolerance. Here is his answer to the question: "Where may the limits lie?"

"Do not touch my private transport even if dangerous smog is unavoidable. Do not cut back my energy spending even if I dirty all the skies of the west and begin the plutonium pile-up. Do not threaten my $12 billion industry, with its 65,000 workers even if vinyl chloride does produce cancer. If my job or my comfort or my free-riding or my rising expectations are threatened, count me out."[12]

Is this a reasonable assessment? If so, what does it suggest about the conditions and forces to which American politicians will be responsive? If it is not a credible assessment, wherein does it err?

The reviewer clearly identified three sensitive areas in which public tolerance of restrictions is severely limited as of now. To the extent that elected executives and legislators are subservient to these limits, they are unlikely to move very decisively to reduce consumption of energy or to force by taxation or other incentives major changes in industrial practices and personal styles of living. However, we are inclined to the view that this is a short-sighted assessment, and that events in this sector, as in others, may shrink timetables that would have seemed reasonable even as recently as the middle 1960s.

Perhaps a little summing up will cast some light on our expectations. There is apparent public support, or at least tolerance, for reduction of the more ubiquitous, disagreeable, and dangerous pollutions. Something similar is occurring, as yet very moderately, with regard to conservation of energy and materials. However, it is difficult to discover much willingness to pay a stiff price in money or inconvenience for protection. Such attitudes are reflected in the speeches and votes of lawmakers and administrators. Elected politicians, in particular, tend to be cautious pragmatists. Predilection for short-term gains, as in the realm of business, permeates the conduct of public affairs. A bird in hand is worth ten in the bush, especially if there is uncertainty as to precisely what is in the bush.

In this respect environmental politics is like all politics, only perhaps a little more so. The normal strategy is to wait and see; perhaps something will turn up. The governing maxim is: don't change very much all at once or too soon; if possible, avoid abruptly disturbing the status quo, even though there is credible evidence that failure to act decisively *now* may magnify both damage and cost later on.

Some of this wait-and-see attitude plainly reflects the notion that environmental hazards cannot possibly be as serious as many ecologists and other specialists contend. A corollary of this skepticism is the notion that environmental agitation is a "passing fad" that will fade away as other fads capture the headlines. Still another corollary is the pervasive, generally unspoken, assumption that Americans can continue to preempt indefinitely one-half of the world's accessible energy—and get away with it.

In our view, these are questionable assumptions. Environmentally linked hazards seem no more likely to fade away than poverty and discrimination are likely to vanish spontaneously. Procrastination may provide a reprieve but not an escape. Though much remains to be learned, enough is already known by now to justify an expectation that environmental deterioration will worsen progressively as long as widely current public attitudes, policies, and practices continue.

It would be easy at this point to retreat into fatalistic pessimism. However, to do so would ignore how much has been achieved within less than two decades, and what is currently in hand or projected.

There are indubitably "sticky" areas as the quotation from the *Economist* above indicated. Most Americans who can afford a car of any kind, from a jalopy to a Cadillac, are not going to yield without stubborn resistance the convenience of private transport, or at least not until the cost of automobiles, annual registration, insurance, maintenance, fuel, and traffic congestion put this amenity beyond reach. Workers' unions in many industries seem likely to continue indefinitely their leaders' tacit alliance with management in order to protect what union officers believe to be job-threatening regulations. Fear of unemployment may continue to persuade thousands of miners and other industrial workers to tolerate risks that threaten to shorten their lives just as surely as inveterate addiction to cigarettes. Mistaken notions, fed by self-serving propaganda, may convince large sections of the public that nuclear-fission power will be cheaper and more abundant than less-hazardous sources of the energy that governs so many aspects of their lives.

These examples, of course, are only fragments of a much larger panorama. However, they do suggest reasonably expectable public resistance to three restrictive changes that today would be widely regarded as intolerable encroachments on the American "way of life." How Americans would react to gradual changes in even these sensitive areas, one can only conjecture. But we are impressed by evidence, both historical and contemporary, that most Americans are more resilient and adaptive than the quoted passage from the *Economist* suggests. At least that is the way we interpret progress already achieved toward a safer and more healthful physical habitat.

The beginnings of the contemporary movement to arrest environmental deterioration can be conveniently dated from the years immediately following World War II. We have indicated some of the pioneers, in chapter 1 and elsewhere: Rachel Carson, Barry Commoner, Paul and Anne Ehrlich, Kenneth Boulding, and many others. Their admonitions were mightily strengthened by disastrous oil spills, blackouts, dam failures, and other so-called acts of God. This concurrence of events, reflecting accelerative disruption of the biosphere, may very well appear to future historians to have been as decisive a historical break, or discontinuity, as the invention and proliferation of nuclear superweapons. It would take a fair-sized book to elaborate this conjecture, and to describe even the more salient items in the accumulating degradation of the earth. We have cited a few exhibits and we review some of them here in this summing up of the unfinished environmental business of America's third century.

We have noted the increasingly rigorous and restrictive regulations imposed on agribusiness, mining, and other industries. We have cited the updating of municipal sanitary systems; we have noted also the increasing scrutiny of military demands and practices, and of other expenditures of chronically deficient public resources. Such data do not necessarily portend a significant future trend, or a substantial break with the past. To date, however, efforts to arrest two centuries and more of waste and pollution add up to a greater achievement than any contemporary observer could reasonably have anticipated in the early post-1945 years.

There is space here to mention only a few exhibits, chosen more or less at random: the court order to the Reserve Mining Company to cease, within a reasonable time, discharging asbestos-laden ore residues into Lake Superior; General Electric's agreement with New York State to cease polluting the Hudson River with poisonous PCB, and to help finance restorative procedures; public and private reactions to the notorious Kepone pollution of Virginia waterways; increasing restrictions on oil drilling and other industrial operations off the continental coasts; the beginnings of pressure to cease turning invaluable croplands into superfluous superhighways and real estate developments; the defeat (at this writing) of an Air Force project to build a fleet of superbombers costing $100 millions or more per plane. One could go on and on, citing scores, perhaps hundreds, of decisions at all levels of government, which, if sustained, will go far toward saving the American physical and social environments from the utter ruination toward which these seemed headed in the flush fifties and sixties.

In retrospect, much of the credit goes obviously to those civic leaders, in and out of government, who achieved enactment of the National Environmental Protection Act of 1969. That historic legislation formed the legal foundation for much that has happened since. The Environmental Protection Agency was built upon it. It provided the legal authority for assaults on pesticides and pollutions of air, water, and land, and for expanded study of ecological systems, and much else of environmental concern, especially during the fruitful administration of Russell E. Train. In addition, the 1969 Act and its supplements opened the way for the technological and environmental assessments that are increasingly required before work on major projects can begin. The act, the agency, dedicated judges, and a varied assortment of civic leaders and organizations brought environmental projects and decisions into public view, exposing hazards that would previously have been closely kept industrial or governmental secrets. Events opened the courts a little wider to suits against polluters, attacked with notable success the common-law doctrine of "burden of proof," and otherwise stimulated the growth of environmental law. Events also set the stage for more rigorous enforcement of standards which, if still insufficient, are miles ahead of traditional enforcement. In sum, it is a fair surmise that environmental legislation and administration, aided by private individuals and organizations, have blocked or forced cancellation of damaging and hazardous projects in numerous fields, though not enough by any tenable ecological standard.

Efforts to arrest environmental deterioration have produced several kinds of effects. As expected there has been some successful defiance of standards and regulations. It has shown up publicly in the marketplace mentality of business-managements preoccupied with short-term profits whatever the longer-term risks. Fines imposed on companies and individuals have rarely been sufficient deterrents. Increasingly, violators of environmental standards have opted for agreement out of court, presumably to minimize adverse publicity. Characteristically, Congress and state legislatures have been "reluctant dragons," especially with money for environmental and social progress. Perhaps the strongest sanction of all may prove in the long run to be the adverse publicity that accompanies many of the more notorious cases.

On the constructive side, hundreds if not thousands of municipalities have received state and federal aid that makes overdue sanitary renovations and other reforms possible. Some business managements have been nudged along by various incentives to do what they ought to do voluntarily in the public interest. Perhaps even more important, the environmental administrative agencies—federal, state, and local—are driving home the message that conservation of energy and materials, and reductions of many pollutions, can save money and, in a little longer run, even increase profits. In the still longer run, this discovery may contribute significantly to a less exploitive attitude toward the limited and shrinking resources of the planet earth.

What has been accomplished thus far, many claim, is only a drop in the bucket. But we shall conjecture in the Epilogue that present accomplishments and ongoing governance point toward a cleaner, quieter, safer, and more healthful habitat for rich and poor alike.

Epilogue
Mainly in the Realm of Conjecture

Dictionaries define an epilogue as a "concluding section that rounds out the design of a literary work." What we have to say in these few remaining pages does round out the design previewed in the Prologue. However, we also venture into deeper waters, since we shall offer some personal conjectures about the unfinished environmental business of America's third century.

We begin by restating some of the premises from which we approach this task. First, we assume that the fate of Americans, as of humankind in general, will continue to depend upon conditions prevailing in the biosphere of the planet earth. We view as sheer fantasy all schemes for transporting some remnant of humankind to permanent colonies in outer space if the earth becomes unfit for human habitation.

Second, we assume that the state of our terrestrial habitat will continue to depend chiefly on prevailing attitudes and activities —how Americans feel toward their country and its future as reflected in what they do and say as they go about daily living, working, and playing.

Third, we further assume that what is done toward environmental repair and protection will continue to be entangled with conflicting attitudes toward nature, toward distribution of income and wealth, toward opportunity and discrimination, and toward a multiplicity of other conditions and forces.

Fourth, we find generally credible the diagnoses of professional ecologists, a few physicists and economists, and others who envisage the possibility that certain current trends, if allowed to continue, could culminate in collapse of industrial society, if not in worse calamities, within a century more or less. We neither anticipate nor exclude such an outcome.

We recognize the destructive potential of thermonuclear war, but also the possibly calamitous consequences of still-expanding energy-intensive industrialism, accidents in biochemical laboratories, worsening imbalance between food and population, and not least, the insidious piecemeal destruction of the life-sustaining biosphere, resulting from the practices of present-day industrialism and the personal life-styles that accompany these.

Even if the statistical odds of overwhelming catastrophe from these or other sources are generally calculated, today, to be minute, much damage has already occurred and some of it is irreversible in either an absolute or a pragmatic sense. Fossil fuels once burned are gone forever. The genetic pool is permanently impoverished by extinction of plant and animal species. Premature death or permanent disablement of human individuals from whatever cause is likewise irreversible. Mental impairment from severe malnutrition in infancy and early childhood may be irreparable. In an operational sense, much of the damage that is technically reparable and many hazards that are technically reducible are not in fact either repaired or reduced, or likely to be. In the well-chosen words of the late Isaiah Bowman, "Man conforms to many defective layouts because it would cost him too much to alter them."[1]

Contrary to some eminent economists, we doubt that stoking the fires of energy-intensive industrialism is a promising prescription for America's third century. This prescription provides only a reprieve at most. If the reprieve continues to be frittered away, the longer-range effect will be merely to shift worsening hazards to generations yet unborn.

We incline to agree with those economists who contend that the conventional growth process rests upon an eroding foundation. We find no ground for believing that pure and applied science and the marketplace can sustain current-style growth indefinitely. The energy cost of getting more energy seems likely to go on rising, and sooner or later the units of energy thus consumed seem likely to overtake the units of new energy obtained. We are impressed that this application of the venerable principle of diminishing returns applies not only to fossil fuels but also to nuclear fission, and perhaps to nuclear fusion as well, if (as rarely occurs) calculations of cost include all relevant items—research, experimentation, capital investment, operating costs, security of plants, price and availability of fuels, security of fuels and residues in transit, and safe disposal of worn-out reactors and spent-fuel residues that remain lethally radioactive virtually forever.

Even so, government and public may opt for this costly and dangerous escape from the necessity of significant conservation, under the misguided impression that something will turn up to make such conservation unnecessary. We have come reluctantly to fear that it may require several major disasters, along with inexorably rising bills for fuel and power and virtually everything else, to pry open enough closed minds, not only in America but in scores of other energy-hungry societies around the world. Economically feasible processes for concentrating large quantities of the continuing massive but diffuse inputs of solar energy may eventually provide less constrictive and dangerous options, but how soon and against how much resistance remains to be seen.

If these are reasonable deductions from present evidence, then, even if the rate of global population growth is lowered more than currently projected, we anticipate that the focus of environmental politics will grudgingly and gradually shift away from predominant emphasis on expanding energy supplies toward more intensive efforts to reduce the demand and consumption of energy—a shift that most politicians, scientists, and probably a majority of their fellow citizens today regard as almost unthinkable.

Even if such a trend does emerge and gains some momentum, we envision no strategy for coping with hunger and continuing degradation of the biosphere unless a drastic reduction of technological military competition is somehow achieved, and the preemption of resources and other disruptive impacts of an economy perpetually on a semi-war footing are correspondingly reduced.

Too exclusive contemplation of these and other obstacles could easily incline one toward fatalistic pessimism, despite the evidences of progress noted on the final pages of chapter 9. Some such vista seems to us clearly implicit in numerous futuristic scenarios. However, three-quarters of a century of living in various American and foreign milieux has not persuaded us that Americans (admitting plenty of exceptions) are as a nation so incurably greedy, and their wants and expectations so rigidly materialistic, that only a police-state regime can arrest the practices that are driving the country toward environmental ruin. The history of American culture is a record of continuous adaptation to change, with more or less continuous intermingling of voluntary choices and imposed restraints.

Adaptation to a changing milieu is manifestly less traumatic when the prospect is for expanding opportunities and more material abundance. How most Americans will react to an increasingly restrictive milieu is a question that no one can answer today. Our own conjecture is that there will be plenty of frustration and perhaps considerable violent resistance, but sufficient resilience to sustain a middle course: some combination of imposed restraints and less coercive incentives in future management of the physical environment. Such a process would be similar to what is occurring today in numerous other sectors of our society.

Moreover, as we shall amplify in a moment, the adaptive process seems less likely to be disorderly if abrupt restrictive changes can be avoided. Part of what we have in mind was expressed more eloquently by the pioneer ecologist Aldo Leopold. In a plea for less drastic and abrupt assaults on the habitat, he said, in 1948: "By and large our present problem is one of attitudes and implements. We are remodeling the Alhambra with a steam shovel [bulldozer, in today's vernacular]. . . . We shall hardly relinquish the shovel, which after all has many good points, but we are in need of gentler and more objective criteria for its successful use. . . . The combined evidence of history and ecology seems to support one general deduction: the less violent the man-made changes [in nature], the greater the probability of successful readjustment."[2]

Our surviving, if somewhat shaken, faith in American capacity to follow Leopold's advice derives in part from our reading of American history, and from some personal observation and experience. As for the latter, we were among the millions who lost their jobs or clung precariously to the bottom rung, but managed somehow to survive without losing faith in their own or their nation's future during the hideous nightmare of the Great Depression of the 1930s, an experience we have discovered to be about as remote and unreal to most young and middle-aged adults today as the Nazi atrocities or the miseries of working people in early industrial England.

During World War II we were among millions who were deprived of new cars and subjected to drastic rationing of gasoline, tires, heating fuel, meat, flour, sugar, clothing, and a great many other things previously taken for granted. Despite cheating, chiseling, and grumbling, there was far more compliance than defiance. To a recently expressed assertion that "the unities of wartime do not justify the inference that in peacetime people will do what they ought to do for the common good," our response is: *Maybe, but not proved.*[3] In retrospect, we are impressed by the resilience of most Americans during the Great Depression, again during World War II, and on numerous other occasions. We are also impressed by the ability of most of our fellow citizens, when hard pressed, to make the best of frustrating situations, even though they do not understand very well the sources of their privations and disrupted modes of living. Our motto is: Don't sell America short!

There is no certainty, of course, that future Americans will respond as most of their great-grandparents did. We are not so naïve as to imagine that America's third century will replicate the second. We suspect that a great deal will depend on the quality of future leadership in government, business, unions, academia, and other fields. Trustworthy as well as trusted civic leadership may well prove to be even more important during an era of subtle, insidious deterioration than in the dramatic collapse of the early thirties, and following the traumatic shock of Pearl Harbor. This is one of the reasons we attach so much importance to leadership in the present context of environmental degradation.

It may be objected that expectations of unlimited economic growth, cultivated from earliest childhood, are hard to change, and that most citizens (including a great many well-educated by current standards) are incapable of assessing either the hazards attributable to exploitive industrialism and latent in numerous scientific and engineering agendas or those caused by living habits of most reasonably prosperous citizens generally. This is not an unreasonable objection. We are impressed by the apparently widening gap between the ways that most nonscientists and most scientists perceive and react to their shared habitat. Such was the essence of C. P. Snow's well-known concept of the "two cultures"—the scientific and the humanistic—that exist side by side with scarcely any communication possible between them.[4]

This dilemma of incommunicability is evident in disputes about weapons research and development, large-scale reliance on nuclear-fission power, automation in industry and transport, use of electronic computers, and much else these days. One may doubt that very many nonscientists will ever comprehend very well the outlook, ethos, and modes of thinking that characterize what is loosely called the scientific subculture. But nonscientists can learn more about the hazards and consequences as well as the putative benefits of avant-garde agendas of pure and applied science. Conversely, scientists can learn a great deal more about the society in which they carry on their work, and especially about the multiple hazards from diverse sources that compete for larger allocations from the grossly insufficient dollars at the disposal of government.

These and other aspects of broader understanding will require a wider field of vision than now prevails in either of the two subcultures, and much greater appreciation of what is politically probable and financially possible. This imperative reevokes some of the questions dealt with in previous chapters. Who will translate the scientific subculture to nonscientists—and who the humanist culture to nonhumanists? Who will determine priorities among competing claimants for insufficient disposable resources? What conditions and forces will determine who gets how much of what is available?

Responsibility for defining the public interest lies in the final reckoning with those who are legally invested with such responsibility. However, they will need additional assistance from many sources—from academia, from business managements, from the public media, and from the all-too-few individuals who can converse with understanding and empathy across the no-man's-land that divides the two subcultures.

It may still be objected that relatively few citizens have reliable means of determining whom to trust, and that recent history has increased distrust of all civic leadership. We do not minimize this objection. It may yet prove to be a disabling handicap in dealing with the unfinished environmental business of America's third century. Moreover ignorance, incompetence, lying, deceit, corruption, and sheer greed at the top are as contagious as measles, and this contagion spreads through many channels.

Men and women in responsible echelons of government and in business, education, and other opinion-influencing roles are inescapably models and exemplars. They set the style not only within their compartmented microenvironments but also in the body politic as a whole. The contagious effects of discreditable behavior have been repeatedly demonstrated, in revelations relating to the Vietnam war, in the Watergate disclosures, and in continuing exposures of bribery and other corruption extending into the higher echelons of domestic government, international statecraft, and the conduct of private business.

Shakespeare put it all together in *Troilus and Cressida*. We refer to Ulysses' rebuke to the feckless Greek king, bogged down in the siege of Troy: "When degree [in today's idiom, *honor, standing,* or *worth*] is shaked/ . . . The enterprise is sick. . . . /

Take but degree away, untune that string,/And, hark! what discord follows."[5]

When deceit and other corruption in business and statecraft are publicly defended by the excuse that "everybody does it"; when it is asserted that too much honesty doesn't pay; when it is widely accepted that corruption is a requisite of success, even of survival, in domestic and international business and statecraft; when there are indications that such an ethos has penetrated deeply into many niches of the society—then there is at least prima facie ground for fearing that Shakespeare was right.

Personally, despite considerable evidence to the contrary, we do not accept quite so gloomy a view of the American condition and prospect. Not everybody "does it." Honest men and women, including many in posts of civic leadership and responsibility, do not always "finish last." We are likewise unimpressed by fatalistic public laments that nothing can be done to improve the muddy ethos that indubitably does infect a good deal of public and private behavior in America today.

Should events prove us wrong, and the cynics right, that fact would give greater plausibility to the more pessimistic scenarios previously summarized. It would do so, we repeat, because predominantly competent, honest, and credible leadership, in business as in government and other professions, is (by our lights) an indispensable condition of getting ahead with the unfinished environmental and societal tasks confronting America today.

We do not anticipate eradication of corruption and deceit from the conduct of public and private affairs. We do not underestimate the difficulties of rearing children to be honorable and responsible adults in a milieu which rewards material success however obtained. We do not minimize the difficulty of dealing with domestic and transnational businesses, and with foreign political regimes, that are permeated with liars, bribers, and other corrupters. We also recognize, by analogy with Gresham's "law" of money, that corruption tends to drive probity out of circulation.

However, despite much evidence to the contrary, we do not regard it as simplistic fantasy to look forward to at least modest improvement in the ethics of public and private affairs. Moreover, any improvement at all will lessen by so much the risk of aborting the unfinished agenda of social and environmental reform. The prospect should brighten still more if certain additional conditions can be met.

We emphasize first the need for wider appreciation of the interrelatedness of our world. This interrelatedness embraces both nonhuman and human phenomena. Many have deplored a widely prevailing sense of detachment from distant conditions and events, even those occurring within our own country. This unconcern was brought sharply into focus as we wrote this final chapter by reports from many parts of the United States that people were saying, "What's New York to me?" in response to that city's power blackout in July 1977 and the accompanying vandalism, looting, and violence.

Second, we sense a comparable need for clearer awareness of the hazards latent in many of the advances in pure and applied science—hazards that are often obscured by self-serving propaganda of those who hunger for larger profits, professional kudos, or other short-term gains.

Third, there is need for a more informed discussion of budgetary priorities at all levels of governance. Which do we need more: an endless succession of more-and-more destructive superweapons or better-educated citizens—a question dramatized by recent reports that sixty times as many dollars are spent equipping each United States soldier as are allocated (at all governmental levels) to educating each American child of school age. Do we need more yachts, Cadillacs, and other luxuries for the rich, or more and better food and housing for the poor and destitute? More private automobiles or better public transportation? More imported oil or less waste of this precious ingredient of nearly everything we use? These are merely samples chosen at random from a list that could be easily extended.

Fourth, there is urgent need for more understanding of the fragility of complex systems. It has been repeatedly demonstrated that if a system *can* fail it will, sooner or later. Yet most Americans still seek salvation by new and more complex technology, without much concern for the human and material costs of systemic failures.

Fifth, perhaps more than anything else, Americans desperately need a less exploitive philosophical posture. Exploitive attitudes and practices worked after a fashion in a pioneer land where natural resources were abundant, population was sparse and scattered, and most of the work was done by human and animal muscles. An exploitive posture becomes increasingly destructive as population increases and is more densely concentrated in industrial areas, as accessible high-grade fuels and other natural resources become less abundant and progressively more expensive, and as technical and social systems become so complex that elaborate fail-safe devices and sophisticated technicians cannot, or at least fail to, prevent recurrent disastrous breakdowns.

Very few Americans would willingly return to preindustrial modes of living. It is a plausible supposition that today's population could not even survive if dependent solely upon the knowledge, skills, and tools of the eighteenth century. In any case, no such solution is envisioned in this discussion. However, a new look at the damage and hazards of industrial gigantism and increasing systemic complexity is definitely an ingredient of this discussion of the context of environmental politics. Under what conditions are bigness and complexity humanly hazardous as well as environmentally destructive? Under what conditions do such conditions set the stage for major disasters? When is *smaller* safer and more reliable?

Thanks primarily to Schumacher, these questions are getting some serious attention.[6] More people are becoming conscious of hazards that inexorably increase with economic and technological complexity, and of what these and related trends are doing to the earth and to those who inhabit it. But only a tiny dent has yet been made in the colossal ignorance and dogmatism that enshroud most discussions of these subjects.

We have noted the difficulty of persuading enough politicians, bureaucrats, businessmen, teachers, and other civic leaders—and citizens in general—that the prospect can possibly be as threatening as a few have depicted. Perpetually rising prices for nearly everything, recurrent shortages of fuel and power, increasing cost and diminishing quality of personal services, recurrent breakdowns of the systems upon which people increasingly depend, perhaps even more spectacular disasters, may be necessary to shake public apathy. In short, what people read, and what they see and hear on television, may be considerably less effective as incentives to reduce waste and other destructive activities than wider experience with recurrent shortages, with illnesses attributable to pollutions, and with other *direct* evidence of their vulnerability to a progressively less healthful habitat.

In response to reiterated assertions that Americans will never relinquish their expectations of making more money and buying more amenities ad infinitum, there is accumulating evidence (most of which gets remarkably little publicity) that millions are already scaling down their materialistic habits and expectations —simply because they can discover no acceptable alternative. Is it unreasonable to speculate that this process of incremental readjustment may gradually, and quite subtly, reshape expectations that many in our midst seem still to consider to be as enduring as the Rock of Gibraltar? What we are mildly suggesting is that the impacts of daily living, reinforced by moderately restrictive standards, and some extension of awareness, may be nudging Americans toward more regard for the ultimate fundamentals of their existence. Such an incremental process might even contribute significantly during the next century to a cultural about-face that, for most people today, seems too visionary and improbable to deserve serious consideration.

Even a slight shift in posture could entail significant consequences. For example, we have recorded our skepticism that present tax structures—federal, state, and local—will ever generate enough revenue to cover the steadily increasing arrears and annual costs of overdue social and environmental reforms, *as long as these costs are added on top of huge allocations for military and other environmentally destructive purposes*. We have also queried whether this dilemma can be resolved by efforts to enlarge the tax base by the route of conventional economic growth. We are persuaded that adequate financing of social and environmental programs will remain beyond reach as long as current allocations of disposable revenues prevail.

If these are reasonable conjectures (and we anticipate their rejection by numerous avant-garde scientists, conventional economists, and hard-line militarists), then an important conclusion emerges for serious consideration: either there will be some shift in attitudes and budgetary priorities, or social and environmental damage and hazards will inexorably grow worse and less manageable.

We do not dispute the need for credible military defense. We are simply stating a conclusion that seems to us unavoidable in the larger context of proliferating vulnerabilities to which Americans and their habitat are increasingly and menacingly subjected. Books, articles, and a bulging file of press clippings tell us that we are not the only ones who perceive this dilemma. Others include eminent scientists, former government officials, retired military professionals, academic scholars in the social and humanistic disciplines, and still others.[7]

We are well on the way to a conviction that no political system—not even one as authoritarian as the Russian—can continue much longer to allocate so large a share of its national product to military and related purposes without progressively weakening the social and physical foundations upon which not merely the power but also the internal vitality and durability of every national polity depends. In short, the ordering of priorities is the core around which environmental policies take shape.

Turning to the choice of strategies, one finds a rich assortment of prescriptions but no consensus. There are, however, a limited number of basic choices. The first, to repeat a point emphasized in chapter 2, is the choice between doing nothing and doing something. If the latter, the second choice is between voluntarism and imposed constraint. If voluntarism is judged to be ineffective in critical issues, imposed constraint can be assigned to either the private or the public sector, or to some combination thereof.

Experience to date suggests that very little can be expected from the profit-oriented private sector, since almost any constraint affects the distribution of income and wealth, especially short-term profits. Since what is done about depletions, pollutions, and systemic disruptions of the biosphere always affects some combination of individuals, groups, or the community as a whole (in some cases beneficially, in others, adversely), the tendency is for environmental repair and protection to gravitate into the public sector—that is, toward the institutions and incumbents explicitly responsible for protecting the public interest, however that interest may be defined. Public authorities can execute this responsibility through various channels and procedures. They can set standards to which the whole community is obligated to conform. They can choose among various modes of obtaining compliance: for example, they can exhort, publicize noncompliance, impose fines, or even send flagrant violators to prison. Or alternatively, they can offer less oppressive incentives, such as, say, direct financial aid, tax relief, depreciation allowances, and still others.

No brief sketch can do justice to the rich variety of options, or to the multiplicity of reasons for choosing one rather than another. We have given some indications in previous chapters of the range of choices that may be effective as well as politically feasible.

During the late 1960s and early 1970s, when the public spotlight was mainly on pollutions, the antigovernment bias of conventional economic theory and of business practice was much in evidence. It was reflected in opposition to direct governmental regulations backed by punitive sanctions. It was likewise implicit in most schemes for maximizing economic incentives to persuade business managements to do what they ought to do for the public good. The predominant version included some form of taxation—euphemistically called "pollution charges"—to induce gross polluters to change their ways and maybe increase profits by doing so.

There was merit in this approach to reduction of pollutions attributable to business practices. However, it was far from a universally acceptable or effective therapy. It was axiomatic that pollution taxes, like other business expenses, would be passed along to consumers in higher prices. Thus, the strategy was as regressive and socially unfair as the flat-rate sales taxes that overburden the poor for the benefit chiefly of the affluent. Furthermore, it requires exercise of public authority to impose and to collect *any* tax. It is also debatable how effective pollution taxes would be against giant corporations, as in the case of General Electric's gross pollution of the Hudson River. Moreover, taxing polluters is a strictly domestic remedy. How, for example, could Congress assess charges against the Chinese government for radioactive fallout upon the United States originating in weapons testing in central Asia?

The merits of any strategy should be judged by such criteria as: How relevant is it to the problem in hand? Can it be effectively administered? Will it worsen the inequities that still plague our society? Within such boundaries, it seems manifestly sensible to depend as much as possible on strategies that simplify administration, maximize private incentives, and minimize punitive sanctions. However, the record suggests that most business managements, if given a free choice, will choose policies and practices that maximize their own profits without much concern for larger social and environmental consequences. Indeed, some spokesmen for business have explicitly asserted that protection of the public interest is not their responsibility but the government's—and then they defend policies that impede effective exercise of public authority.

Public authorities can exercise their responsibility in many ways. One illustrative example is the combination of sticks and carrots evolved in modernizing antiquated municipal sewerage systems. The state government can prohibit additional sewer connections (often a severe deterrent to new building) until the municipality's sanitary system is adequately enlarged or renovated. Then the state and federal governments can provide financial aid (sometimes nearly the full cost) to induce the municipal government to do its job, so that new building can be resumed. It would require a sizable volume to describe the manifold combinations of sticks and carrots employed to expedite the reduction of scores of kinds of pollutions that contribute to deterioration of the physical habitat.

When in the mid-1970s attention shifted abruptly to shortages of energy, the strategy problem exhibited a different face. Antigovernment bias was somewhat muted. Since the American public as well as particular industries are heavily dependent upon imported oil and numerous essential materials, governmental intervention to sustain imports and combat steeply rising prices was generally welcomed. Since the development of new energy sources and synthetic substitutes for increasingly expensive raw materials requires large outlays for research and development, and since much of this research and development entails considerable risk of no ultimate profit, grants from public funds are heavily in demand. But so far as we can discover, the recipients of this public support are as resistant as ever to governmental regulations pertaining to use, accounting, and so forth.

For these and other reasons, continued progression toward a safer and more healthful habitat seems to us to require longer-range planning, wider-angle vision, a stronger sense of public responsibility, and other changes in attitudes and practices than can be reasonably expected from profit-oriented, predominantly exploitive business managements.

Moreover in many instances only government can mobilize the necessary resources. Only government commands the police-power necessary in the final reckoning to deal with intransigent defiance of standards. Only government can determine priorities among competing claims from a multiplicity of sources. Only government can allocate chronically insufficient disposable resources. Only government can protect the public interest against some forms of exploitive private business practices. Hence we envision no prospect whatever that the role of public authority will diminish in the continuing struggles over energy and other natural resources, and over pollutions and resultant disruptions of the biosphere. It seems far more likely that the government's role will expand still further in dealing with damage and hazards from these sources.

In reaching this conclusion, we do not underestimate the institutional and personal deficiencies of all governments. There is no certainty that political executives, legislative bodies, administrative agencies, and the courts will be either trusted or trustworthy. But we never let ourselves forget that public authorities are, by definition and by legal investiture, responsible for protecting the public interest. And this conclusion is unavoidable however the public interest is defined or how well or poorly it is defended.

The above paragraphs are neither a plea for nor a defense of the expanding role of public authority in maintaining a decently livable habitat. Nor do we minimize the limited capability of our government and all others to fulfill this mission unilaterally in our politically fragmented tribalistic world.

However, by no means all environmentally linked damage and hazards are of foreign origin, or involve difficult negotiations with regimes bent on industrialization and other ways of obtaining a larger share of the earth's developed wealth. The unfinished business of environmental protection includes many problems manageable within the boundaries of American space, jurisdiction, and effective influence and power. As many experts have reiterated, dependence on imported oil and other essentials can be greatly reduced by more courageous and persistent efforts to reduce waste. Many pollutants of air, water, and land are entirely or mainly of local origin. Some of the residual systemic disruptions can be reduced if not eradicated by unilateral action.

Still, there remains a refractory core of environmental problems beyond unilateral reach. Some monitoring and other collaborative projects have been started, but many baffling puzzles remain unsolved. These are puzzles that derive in considerable degree from the earth's political fragmentation, but also from regional and global differences in knowledge and outlook, in uneven geographical distribution of essential resources and populations, in technical and economic levels of development, in hunger and affluence, and in many other differentiating features of the more than 145 sovereign polities that compose the international order.

It should be clear by now that we do not anticipate either rapid or radical progress toward a cleaner, quieter, safer, and more healthful America. We strongly doubt that very many of our fellow citizens will climb Pike's Peak before breakfast, especially since there is considerable uncertainty about the menu awaiting them at the summit. However, upward progress, though uneven and recurrently stalled, is discernible. We anticipate that it will continue through America's third century. But, as repeatedly emphasized in these pages, a good deal will depend on the prevailing outlook and ethos. It is becoming increasingly difficult to exclude at least some of the more harmful consequences from the consciousness of millions who have previously given this source of damage and hazard little or no serious attention. We would today give at least even odds that the course of events will sustain progressively tightening standards and a greater degree of general if grudging compliance thereto.

However, such progress will require greater and more widespread understanding of the "limits of the earth." Such understanding, in turn, will require competent, candid, trustworthy, and trusted civic leadership in and out of officialdom. Progress will also entail continuing compromises between liberty and imposed constraint. These compromises will seem too radical to some and too conservative to others. Hence it seems likely that few clear-cut choices will be forthcoming. Piecemeal remedies for specific, widely perceived damage and hazards will probably continue to be the norm. The anticipated pattern of statecraft: a few short steps from year to year, with recurrent backsliding.

To objections that such a process will fall far short of keeping pace with the glacierlike drift toward ruination of the earth, any response today can be no more than conjectural. Ours is that incremental patchwork may add up to significant improvement during the next century. The basis for this expectation is both the record of the recent past and the repeated evidence of resilience of American culture to environmental change.

In sum, then, if thermonuclear war or other abrupt irreversible catastrophe is avoided—admittedly a rather large *if*—piecemeal adjustments, though certain to be an untidy process, seem likely to be more effective in the aggregate than many skeptics currently concede. Whether incremental adjustments, or any other politically feasible strategy, will be sufficient to maintain a decently livable physical habitat—for rich and poor, young and elderly—is, of course, a still unanswerable question that gives continuing concern to everyone who gropes for direction in the intellectual and emotional as well as physical smog of this transitory era.

A few years ago Joseph Wood Krutch, dedicated naturalist as well as eminent literary critic, concluded a little book about the Grand Canyon with the conjecture that "the generation now living may well be that which will make the irrevocable decision whether or not America will continue to be for centuries the one great nation which had the foresight to preserve an important part of its heritage."[8]

Anyone who reads that book discovers quickly that Krutch had more on his mind than preservation of a vast natural monument. His parallel larger concern was with the innumerable human activities that were, and continue to be, despoiling the magnificent country that presently living Americans have inherited, and which they will pass on (in good condition, one hopes) to their children and grandchildren who in turn will bequeath it to their posterity.

Notes

Prologue

1. From opening paragraph of H. M. Tomlinson, *The Sea and the Jungle* (New York: Modern Library, 1928), a classic travelogue of a voyage in the early 1900s.

2. *The Limits of the Earth* is the title of a pioneering book by Fairfield Osborn (Boston: Little, Brown & Co., 1953).

3. *The Politics of Environmental Concern* is the apt title of a book by Walter A. Rosenbaum, written from the perspective of academic political science (New York: Praeger Publishers, 1973).

4. The long neglect of environmental subjects by academic political scientists is verified in the voluminous *Environment: A Bibliography of Social Science and Related Literature*, prepared by Denton E. Morrison, Kenneth E. Hornback, and W. Keith Warner for the Office of Research and Monitoring, U.S. Environmental Protection Agency (Washington, D.C.: Government Printing Office, 1973). This bibliography confirms that Lynton K. Caldwell (Indiana University) was preeminent among academic political scientists in giving serious attention, prior to the 1970s, to environmental legislation and administration. The roster of an interdisciplinary conference, "Man's Role in Changing the Face of the Earth," (1956), sponsored by the Wenner-Gren and National Science foundations, included no political scientists. Two years later the conference "Future Environments of North America," sponsored by the Conservation Foundation, included only one, Professor Caldwell.

5. The primary reference here is to the work performed and/or sponsored by Richard A. Falk (international law, Princeton) and Cyril E. Black (director of the Center of International Studies, Princeton). In the present context we especially recommend Falk's early work, *This Endangered Planet* (New York: Random House, 1971), and his more recent book, *A Study of Future Worlds* (New York: Free Press, 1975). There are also many relevant essays in the five-volume symposium edited by Falk and Black, *The Future of the International Legal Order* (Princeton, N.J.: Princeton University Press, 1969–), especially vol. 4, *The Structure of the International Environment*.

6. Barry Commoner, *The Closing Circle* (New York: Alfred Knopf, 1971), p. 33.

Chapter 1

1. The title of this chapter is borrowed from the title of Fairfield Osborn, *Our Plundered Planet* (Boston: Little, Brown & Co., 1948).

2. For a profusely illustrated, nontechnical review of what is known about

4. Nicholas Wade, quoting the biologist Robert L. Sinsheimer, in "Recombinant DNA: A Critic Questions the Right to Free Inquiry," *Science*, October 15, 1976, pp. 303–6, quotation from p. 306.

5. John C. Cobb, letter to *Science*, November 12, 1976, p. 674.

6. *Science*, October 15, 1976, p. 306.

7. An oil company executive to editor, *Consumer Reports* 39 (May 1974): 425.

8. "Scholars Favor Global Growth," *New York Times*, April 13, 1976, quoting John R. Bunting, chairman of the First Pennsylvania Corporation.

9. David Finn, "The Business of Business Is Not Just Business," *New York Times*, June 28, 1975, op. ed.; John W. Hill, ibid., October 6, 1976, op. ed.

10. Gladwin Hill, the *New York Times*'s well-informed, fair, and sophisticated commentator on environmental news, seems to be less pessimistic. "With Major Exceptions, Pollution Controls Are Working: Industry Is Finally Cleaning Up after Itself," *New York Times*, October 17, 1976.

11. Henry C. Wallich, "A World without Growth," *New York Times*, February 12, 1972, op. ed. Dr. Wallich was formerly professor of economics at Yale.

12. Richard M. Pfeffer, "When the Niceties Go," and "Welcome Aboard. You're Fired," *New York Times*, April 30 and May 2, 1975, both op. ed.

13. See, for example, a derisive review-article by Burton G. Malkiel, "What to Do about the End of the World," *New York Times Book Review*, January 26, 1975.

14. Probably the economist most often cited on the economic implications of the finite earth is Kenneth Boulding. One of his early sorties into this economic-environmental thicket was his short but widely quoted essay, "The Economics of the Coming Spaceship Earth," in Henry Jarrett, ed., *Environmental Quality in a Growing Economy* (Baltimore, Md.: Johns Hopkins Press, 1966), pp. 3–14. Other critics of the growth orthodoxy include Nicholas Georgescu-Roegen, in particular his essay "Energy and Economic Myths," *Southern Economic Journal* 41 (January 1975): 347–81; Herman E. Daley et al., *Toward a Steady-State Economy* (San Francisco: W. H. Freeman Co., 1973); and exchanges between K. William Kapp and Wilfred Beckerman: Kapp, "Environmental Disruption and Social Costs: A Challenge to Economics," *Kyklos* (Basel) 23 (1970): 833–48; Beckerman, "Environmental Policy and the Challenge to Economic Theory," *Social Science Information* (Paris) 11, no. 1 (1972): 7–15; Kapp, "Social Costs, Neoclassical Economics, Environmental Planning: A Reply," ibid., pp. 17–28.

15. Marshall I. Goldman, "The Convergence of Environmental Disruption," *Science*, October 2, 1970, pp. 37–42. Others concur: for example, Barry Commoner, *The Closing Circle* (New York: Alfred A. Knopf, 1971), p. 278.

16. For a brief sketch of the infiltration of ecological concepts into humanistic studies, and of what social scientists and humanists have done with these ideas, see our *An Ecological Paradigm for the Study of International Politics*, Research Monograph no. 30 (Princeton: Center of International Studies, 1968), pp. 22–26.

17. Paul B. Sears, "Ecology: A Subversive Subject," *Bioscience* 14 (July 1964): 11–13, quotation from p. 12.

18. Commoner, *Closing Circle*, pp. 32, 33, 39, 41, 45.

19. Among those who apparently subscribe to one or both of the additional generalizations, the following are representative samples: biologists René Dubos and Paul R. and Anne H. Ehrlich; physicist John P. Holdren; economists Kenneth Boulding, Nicholas Georgescu-Roegen, E. F. Schumacher, and Herman E. Daley; the systems theorists and other specialists who contributed to *The Limits*

to Growth and *Mankind at the Turning Point* sponsored by the Club of Rome research program.

20. Professional ecologists may find flaws in this nonprofessional attempt to summarize their basic model. For professional descriptions of ecological models and processes, see, for example, Edward J. Kormondy, *Concepts of Ecology* (Englewood Cliffs, N.J.: Prentice-Hall, 1969); Eugene P. Odum, *Fundamentals of Ecology*, 3d ed. (Philadelphia: W. B. Saunders Co., 1971).

21. René Dubos, "The Human Landscape," lecture delivered in the Department of State, December 8, 1968. Privately circulated by the author.

22. Eugene Rabinowitch, "Living Dangerously in the Age of Science," *Bulletin of the Atomic Scientists*, January 1972, pp. 5–8, quotation from p. 7.

23. Barbara Ward, "The End of an Epoch," *Economist* (London), May 27, 1972, pp. 66–76, quotation from p. 71.

24. Garrett Hardin, "To Trouble a Star: The Cost of Intervention in Nature," *Bulletin of the Atomic Scientists*, January 1970, pp. 17–20, quotation from p. 17.

25. Frank W. Taussig, *Principles of Economics* (New York: Macmillan Co., 1912), 1:5. Other economic textbooks then and since, until very recently, have (with possibly a few exceptions) taken the same position. Even the *International Encyclopedia of the Social Sciences* (New York: Crowell Collier and Macmillan, 1968) gives scarcely any attention to the social costs of so-called free goods.

26. On applications of scientific methods in ecological analysis, see Hardin, "To Trouble a Star," p. 20; also Odum, *Fundamentals of Ecology*, especially chaps. 1–10; and Kormondy, *Concepts of Ecology*, passim.

27. René Dubos, *So Human an Animal* (New York: Charles Scribner's Sons, 1968), p. 27; Barbara Ward, "End of an Epoch," p. 71; E. F. Schumacher, *Small Is Beautiful: Economics as if People Mattered* (New York: Harper & Row, 1973), p. 115; Eugene P. Odum, "The Emergence of Ecology as a New Integrative Discipline," *Science*, March 25, 1977, pp. 1289–93, quotation from p. 1292; Commoner quoted by Luther J. Carter, "Development of the Poor Nations," *Science*, March 7, 1969, pp. 1046–48, quotation from p. 1048.

28. Paul Shepard and Daniel McKinley, eds., *The Subversive Science: Essays toward an Ecology of Man* (Boston: Houghton Mifflin Co., 1969), pp. 1–10.

29. Paul Shepard, "The Environment," review article in *New York Times Book Review*, August 30, 1970.

30. Eugene P. Odum, *Ecology* (New York: Holt, Rinehart & Winston, 1963), p. 109.

31. Schumacher, *Small Is Beautiful*, p. 13.

32. For a vigorous, if not totally cynical, defense of short-term benefits and gains, see Donald G. MacRae, "The Rational Animal's Map," *New Statesman* (London), May 10, 1974, pp. 662–63.

33. F. Fraser Darling, "The Ecological Approach to the Social Sciences," reprinted from the *American Scientist* 39 (April 1951) in Shepard and McKinley, *The Subversive Science*, pp. 316–27, quotation from p. 327.

34. Boulding, "Economics of Coming Spaceship Earth," p. 11.

Chapter 4

1. This tentative estimate, the most credible that we have discovered, came from a panel on "ecological effects" in the "Study of Critical Environmental Problems," subtitle of a colloquium sponsored by the Massachusetts Institute of Technology, entitled *Man's Impact on the Global Environment* (Cambridge: M. I. T.

Press, 1970), pp. 118–19. Note: this study was not related to the "limits to growth" project, sponsored by the Club of Rome, but was domiciled at M. I. T. during the same period.

2. Amory B. Lovins, "World Energy Strategies: The Case for Long-Term Planning, Part II," *Bulletin of the Atomic Scientists*, June 1974, pp. 38–50, quotation from p. 41; also, by same author, "Energy Strategy: The Road Not Taken," *Foreign Affairs* 55 (October 1976): 65–96.

3. The outlook for energy conservation brightened somewhat after President Carter took office, but it is too early at this writing to predict how the president's proposals will fare in Congress, in the financial and industrial communities, and among citizens generally.

4. The critique by Kaysen was addressed to Donella H. Meadows et al., *The Limits to Growth* (New York: Universe Books, 1972).

5. Carl Kaysen, "The Computer that Printed Out W*O*L*F," *Foreign Affairs* 50 (July 1972): 660–68, quotation from p. 663.

6. Emile Benoit, "The Coming Age of Shortages," *Bulletin of the Atomic Scientists*, January 1976, pp. 7–55, quotation from p. 8.

7. A. B. Lovins, "World Energy Strategies, Part I," *Bulletin of the Atomic Scientists*, May 1974, p. 17.

8. E. F. Schumacher, *Small Is Beautiful* (New York: Harper & Row, 1973), p. 15.

9. Nicholas Georgescu-Roegen, "Energy and Economic Myths," *Southern Economic Journal* 41 (January 1975): 347–81, quotation from p. 354.

10. Wilson Clark, "It Takes Energy to Get Energy," *Smithsonian*, December 1974, pp. 84–90, quotation from p. 85; James P. Sterba, "Second Thoughts on Shale," *New York Times*, November 3, 1974.

11. Anne P. Carter, "Applications of Input-Output Analysis to Energy Problems," *Science*, April 19, 1974, pp. 325–29, quotation from p. 329. This issue of *Science* is devoted entirely to varied aspects of the then acute energy crisis.

12. Harrison Brown, "Technological Denudation," in William L. Thomas, Jr., ed., *Man's Role in Changing the Face of the Earth* (Chicago: University of Chicago Press, 1956), pp. 1023–32, quotation from p. 1030.

13. Brown, "Human Materials Production as a Process in the Biosphere," in *Biosphere* (San Francisco: W. H. Freeman & Co., 1970), pp. 117–24, quotation from p. 124 (italics added). This is one of 11 articles reprinted from the September 1970 issue of *Scientific American* as a book.

14. "Day of Reckoning," R. F. *Illustrated* (newsletter of Rockefeller Foundation), December 1976.

15. Kenneth E. Boulding, "No Second Chance for Man," in *The Crisis of Survival*, ed. by the editors of the *Progressive* and the College Division of Scott, Foresman and Co. (New York: William Morrow & Co., 1970), pp. 160–71, quotation from p. 164.

16. Alvin M. Weinberg, "Social Institutions and Nuclear Energy," *Science*, July 7, 1972, pp. 27–34, quotation from p. 33.

17. Richard A. Falk, letter to *New York Times*, June 28, 1976.

18. Alvin M. Weinberg, "The Many Dimensions of Scientific Responsibility," *Bulletin of the Atomic Scientists*, November 1976, pp. 21–24.

19. Lovins, "Case for Long-Term Planning," p. 45.

20. Cited risks and part of the argument summarized in this paragraph are from testimony presented to a committee of the California state legislature, as reported editorially in *Scientific American*, June 1976, p. 48.

21. Schumacher, *Small Is Beautiful*, p. 18.

22. For nontechnical explanations of these obstructive legal doctrines, see Norman J. Landau and Paul D. Rheingold, *The Environmental Law Handbook* (New York: Ballantine Books, 1971), and Joseph L. Sax, *Defending the Environment* (New York: Alfred Knopf, 1971).

23. Chief Justice Stanley Mosk, California Supreme Court, is reported to have said in a public address that he "deplored the fact that courts . . . [have] been 'throwing monumental roadblocks in the path of effective use of class actions.'" Gladwin Hill in *New York Times*, February 8, 1976.

24. *New York Times*, October 4, 1974.

25. *Science*, July 18, 1975, p. 175.

26. Joseph F. Coates, "In Defense of Technology Assessment," *New York Times*, Sunday Business Supplement, May 13, 1973; also, same author, "Future Societal Perspectives," *International Interactions* 1 (1974): 207–12.

Chapter 5

1. Reported on New Jersey page of Jersey edition of *New York Times*, May 1, 1974.

2. For example, our "The Dilemma of Rising Demands and Insufficient Resources," *World Politics* 20 (July 1968): 660–93, especially pp. 684ff.

3. For example, Robert L. Heilbroner, "Phase II of the Capitalist System," *New York Times Magazine*, November 29, 1971, p. 90.

4. We were informed confidentially that flushing garbage down the toilets became increasingly prevalent during the final days of the 1968 Sanitation Workers' strike in New York City, and that this practice threatened to block the entire sewerage system of the vast city. Had this occurred, our informant asserted, it might have become imperative to evacuate most of the city's millions of inhabitants. Our response—"How and to where?"

5. As reported in the *Economist* (London), March 23, 1974, p. 56.

6. *New York Times*, July 24, 1974. For a discussion of various proposals to cope with the problem of government-employee strikes, see Harry H. Wellington and Ralph K. Winter, Jr., *The Unions and the Cities* (Washington, D.C.: Brookings Institution, 1971).

7. *New York Times*, December 12, 1974.

8. J. Calvin Giddings, "World Population, Human Disaster, and Nuclear Holocaust," *Bulletin of the Atomic Scientists*, September 1973, pp. 21–50, quotation from pp. 45, 46. The author is professor of chemistry, University of Utah.

9. *New York Times*, June 5, 1971.

10. L. Douglas DeNike, "Radioactive Malevolence," *Bulletin of the Atomic Scientists*, February 1974, pp. 16–20; also Russell V. Lee, "When Insanity Holds the Scepter," *New York Times*, April 12, 1974, op. ed.

11. D. V. Segre and A. H. Adler, "The Ecology of Terrorism," *Survival* (London), July/August 1973, pp. 178–83, quotation from p. 181.

12. Ralph E. Lapp, "The Ultimate Blackmail," *New York Times Magazine*, February 4, 1973.

13. Theodore Taylor's career has evolved from weapons-designing to one of warning the world about the hazards of nuclear theft and terrorism. Present reference is to an interview reported in the *Trenton* (N.J.) *Sunday Times Advertiser*, December 9, 1973.

14. Allen V. Kneese, "The Faustian Bargain," *Resources* (Washington, D.C.: Resources for the Future, September 1973), pp. 1–5. The literature attacking and

defending development of fast-breeder plutonium reactors is much too voluminous to cite extensively here.

15. Giddings, "Nuclear Holocaust," p. 23.

16. John Gofman (nuclear physicist), "Nuclear Briefing," *Harper's Magazine*,
April 1974, p. 110.

17. Karl W. Deutsch, "New National Interests," *New York Times*, November
22, 1974, op. ed.

18. Classical antecedents of these contemporary symptoms of community
erosion are brilliantly expounded by James J. Helms, professor of classics, Ober-
lin College, in "Social Stress and Individualism in the Hellenistic World," *Ober-
lin Alumni Magazine*, September/October 1974, pp. 6–11.

19. Vance Packard, *A Nation of Strangers* (New York: Pocket Books, 1974),
pp. 6, 12.

Chapter 6

1. Ruth B. Russell et al., *Air, Water, Earth, Fire* (San Francisco: Sierra Club,
1974).

2. Edith B. Weiss, "Weather as a Weapon," in *Air, Water, Earth, Fire*, pp.
51–62; and, same author, "Weather Control: An Instrument for War?" *Survival*
(London), March/April, 1975, pp. 64–68.

3. Frank Barnaby, "Environmental Warfare," *Bulletin of the Atomic Scientists*,
May 1976, pp. 37–43, especially p. 38.

4. Frank Barnaby, ed., *World Armament and Disarmament* (Stockholm: International Peace Research Institute, 1976). The evidence presented in this report is
summarized in the June 1976 issue of the *Bulletin of the Atomic Scientists*, pp.
25–32. On economic costs of armaments, see also Seymour Melman, *The Permanent War Economy* (New York: Simon and Schuster, 1974).

5. Harold and Margaret Sprout, "The Dilemma of Rising Demands and Insufficient Resources," *World Politics* 20 (July 1968): 660–93, especially pp. 667–68.

6. Milton Leitenberg, "Notes on the Diversion of Resources for Military Purposes in Developing Nations," *Journal of Peace Research*, 1976, no. 2, pp. 111–16,
quotation from p. 112; Barnaby, "World Armament," *Bulletin of the Atomic Scientists*, June 1976, pp. 25, 26, 29.

7. William Epstein, "The Proliferation of Nuclear Weapons," *Scientific American*, April 1975, pp. 18–33, quotation from p. 18.

8. D. V. Segre and A. H. Adler, "The Ecology of Terrorism," *Survival* (London), July/August 1973, pp. 178–83, quotation from p. 181.

9. Mihajlo Mesarovic and Eduard Pestel, *Mankind at the Turning Point* (New
York: E. P. Dutton & Co., 1974), p. 69. The authors are systems analysts associated respectively with Case Western Reserve University and the Technical
University (Hannover, Germany). Their book is one of the major reports from
the research program sponsored by the Club of Rome.

10. Bernard T. Feld, "The Menace of a Fission Power Economy," *Bulletin of
the Atomic Scientists*, April 1974, pp. 32–34, quotation from p. 33. The author,
a nuclear physicist, is editor of the periodical.

11. Paul L. Leventhal, "Plutonium for Peace, Maybe," *New York Times*, July
14, 1976, op. ed. The author is special counsel to the Senate Subcommittee on
Reorganization, Research, and International Organizations. Many others have
spoken to similar effect—among them, David E. Lillienthal, "If This Continues,
the Cockroach Will Inherit the Earth," *New York Times*, June 20, 1975, op. ed.

12. C. Fred Bergsten, "The Threat from the Third World," reprint no. 268,

Brookings Institution, Washington; reprinted from *Foreign Policy*, no. 11, Summer 1973: quoted passages from pp. 107–9 of original.

13. Ragaei Mallakh, letter to *New York Times*, April 6, 1974.

14. Marshall Goldman, "Pollutions: International Complications," *Environmental Affairs* 2 (Spring 1972): 1–15, quotations from pp. 3, 8.

15. *Man's Impact on the Global Environment: Report of the Study of Critical Environmental Problems* (Cambridge: M. I. T. Press, 1970), pp. 224, 253.

16. An admittedly improbable scenario by biologists Dennis Pirages and Paul R. Ehrlich speculates on the worldwide consequences if China should attain the American level of economic consumption per capita: "If All Chinese Had Wheels," *New York Times*, March 16, 1972, op. ed.

17. Most economists and entrepreneurs will doubtless take issue with our formulation of energy/materials options, preferring less heterodox analyses such as, for example, Marion L. Clawson, "Economic Development and Environmental Impact: International Aspects," *Social Science Information* (Paris) 10, no. 4 (1971): 23–43.

18. From *Encyclopedia Britannica*, 11th ed., 1911, 6:779–80.

19. W. Stanford Reid, *Economic History of Great Britain* (New York: Ronald Press, 1954), p. 42.

Chapter 7

1. Garrett Hardin, "To Trouble a Star: The Cost of Intervention in Nature," *Bulletin of the Atomic Scientists*, January 1970, pp. 17–19, quotation from p. 18.

2. Anyone skeptical of the hazards implicit in genetic engineering should read recent and current articles on this subject in the prestigious journal *Science*, weekly voice of the American Association for the Advancement of Science. A popular but (in our judgment) fair and competent assessment is Liebe F. Cavalieri, "New Strains of Life—or Death," *New York Times Magazine*, August 22, 1976. The author is a member of the Sloan-Kettering Institute for Cancer Research, and also professor of biochemistry at Cornell University Graduate School of Medical Scientists.

3. David W. Fisher, "On the Problem of Measuring Environmental Benefits and Costs," *Social Science Information* (Paris) 13, no. 2 (1974):95–105.

4. Allen V. Kneese, "The Faustian Bargain," in *Resources* (Washington, D.C.: Resources for the Future, September 1973), pp. 1–5, quotation from p. 5.

5. For example, *Second Annual Report of the Council on Environmental Quality* (Washington, D.C.: Government Printing Office, 1971), especially pp. 108ff.

Chapter 8

1. Harold and Margaret Sprout, "The Dilemma of Rising Demands and Insufficient Resources," *World Politics* 20 (July 1968):660–93.

2. Leonard A. Lecht, *Goals, Priorities, and Dollars* (New York: Free Press, 1966), p. 53.

3. The expectation of material change for the better contrasts strongly with the expectation in preindustrial society, where social change was not expected. Peter Laslette, *The World We Have Lost* (New York: Charles Scribner's Sons, 1965), p. 4.

4. Fairfield Osborn, *The Limits of the Earth* (Boston: Little, Brown & Co., 1953), a sequel to the same author's *Our Plundered Planet* (Boston: Little, Brown & Co., 1948).

5. In emphasizing this growth of politicization we are not forgetting the continuing plight of those in the categories of near and total destitution. However,

even migrant workers and immigrant field laborers are acquiring rights and benefits denied to skilled craftsmen in earlier stages of industrialization.

6. The distinction between support of the military establishment and of military-related purposes is between funds appropriated directly to the Department of Defense and those allocated to strengthen client regimes and for other purposes associated with the expanded concept of military security.

7. The most thorough analyses of budgetary inflexibility are the annual volumes, sponsored by the Brookings Institution, under the general title, *Setting National Priorities*. The most recent issue that we have seen deals with the Ford administration's proposed budget for fiscal 1976–1977; it was prepared by Barry M. Blechman, Edward M. Gramlich, and Robert W. Hartman (Washington: Brookings Institution, 1975). Many of the data for these and other estimates are from the annual *U.S. Budget in Brief* and the *Statistical Abstract of the United States* (Washington: Government Printing Office). A more speculative analysis, entitled *Setting National Priorities: The Next Ten Years*, prepared by Henry Owen and Charles L. Schultze, was published in 1976 by the Brookings Institution.

8. For an assessment in the specific context of environmental legislation and administration, see Lynton K. Caldwell, "Achieving Environmental Quality: Is Our Present Governmental Organization Adequate?" in Leslie L. Roos, ed., *The Politics of Ecosuicide* (New York: Holt, Rinehart & Winston, 1971) and numerous other contributions to the same symposium. We also suggest James O'Connor, *The Fiscal Crisis of the State* (New York: St. Martin's Press, 1973). For a severe indictment of governmental structures and priorities, we recommend Duane Lockard, *The Perverted Priorities of American Politics* (New York: Macmillan Co., 1971).

9. We make a general statement of the effect of adding state and local expenditures, but provide no statistical review. This additional dimension is covered in the easily available analysis by the research team (Owen and Schultze) at the Brookings Institution that prepared *Setting National Priorities: The Next Ten Years*, esp. chap. 9.

10. From President Eisenhower's address to the American Society of Newspaper Editors, April 16, 1953. In fairness it must be noted that the president was not proposing unilateral arms limitation, but rather was making a plea toward a fresh thrust toward international limitation afforded by the death of Stalin and the then pending armistice in Korea. We are indebted to Brigadier General Douglas Kinnard, ret., now professor at the University of Vermont, for bringing this item to our attention.

11. Robert L. Heilbroner, "Priorities for the Seventies," *Saturday Review*, January 3, 1970, pp. 17–19, quotation on p. 17. For an even stronger critique, see Seymour Melman, *The Permanent War Economy* (New York: Simon & Schuster, 1974), and other books and articles by the same author.

12. Michael T. Yarymovych, "Defense Spending: Lower and Lower," *New York Times*, December 5, 1973, op. ed.

13. All data in Figures 2, 3, and 4 are from governmental sources expressed in current dollars. We have discovered that making allowances for continuing inflation and for variations resulting from rises and dips in the GNP from various causes would complicate the point that these figures are designed to illuminate. The thorough and much more elaborate analyses and figures in the Brookings reports on estimated budgetary priorities do take into account a broader spectrum of variables.

14. All estimates for 1977 are from the *U.S. Budget in Brief: Fiscal 1977* (Was ington, D.C.: Government Printing Office).

15. *Environmental Quality: The First Annual Report of the Council on Envir mental Quality* (Washington, D.C.: Government Printing Office, 1970), p. 319.

16. *U.S. Budget in Brief: Fiscal 1973*, p. 53.

17. As reported in the *New York Times*, January 23, 1977.

18. Commenting on recent trends in military and human-resources budg of the federal government, economist Charles L. Schultze (who became Pr dent Carter's economic advisor in 1977) asserted: "Whatever the course of fense spending may be in the next decade, it is virtually certain that its shar GNP cannot continue to shrink at the same pace" (*The Next Ten Years*, p. 3 Events may or may not confirm this conjecture. In any case, the analysis f which the sentence is quoted was addressed less to the comparisons with wl we are concerned than with allegations that Washington's expenditures consuming progressively larger shares of the GNP. On this latter issue, it w be difficult to fault the Brookings research team. Using a "baseline budget" (removing the bulge attributable to the Vietnam war, and the unusual rise du 1975 in such programs as unemployment compensation, food stamps, we payments, etc.) and a "non-recession" GNP (i.e., corrected for "these ab tions" by assuming a constant unemployment rate of 5 percent, subtractin; incremental costs of the Vietnam war, etc.), the analysis concludes tha "overall level of federal spending has risen less sharply relative to the si the national economy" than the unadjusted figures seem to indicate, bei percent between 1965 and 1975 as against 18 percent from 1955 to 1965. In t of constant dollars, between 1965 and 1977, "real federal outlays will have g at approximately the same rate as real GNP. But this equality in real gr rates, when combined with the faster increase in prices for federal expendi [which are predominantly for services, the cost of which "tend to rise faste1 the prices of goods"] than for GNP as a whole, has caused the share of tot tional income flowing to the federal government to rise to about 20 perce current dollars (*The Next Ten Years*, pp. 327, 328, 331). We have inserte rather complicated summary of the method used by the Brookings analy cause it does have some bearing on comparative trends in federal spend the federal government continues to rely on voluntary military service, a1 requires perpetually rising pay scales and fringe benefits to attract su! volunteers, and if the Defense Department is permitted to continue pro more sophisticated and expensive weapons systems, then it does seem that the military budget will become still more difficult to control. This a related question of priorities among military, human-resources, and er mental demands will tighten the already constrictive dilemma of gros sufficient disposable revenues, with consequences to which we shall re later chapters.

19. See, in particular, Seymour Melman, *The Permanent War Economy: can Capitalism in Decline* (New York: Simon & Schuster, 1974).

20. George Liska, *Imperial America* (Baltimore: Johns Hopkins Un Press, 1967), p. 106.

21. R. S. Lewis, "End of Apollo: The Ambiguous Epic," *Bulletin of th(Scientists*, December 1972, pp. 39–44, quotation from p. 43.

22. Lawrence F. O'Brien, "The Ecology of the Slums," *New York Tin* gust 21, 1971, op. ed.

23. From Whitney Young's syndicated column; paraphrased here from the *Trenton* (N.J.) *Evening Times*, February 16, 1970. Compared with many statements with the same thrust, Young's was a model of sobriety; compare, for example, the slashing attack on environmental programs by Richard Newhouse, *In Defense of People* (New York: Macmillan Co., 1971); and for an even more savage outburst, the exhibit quoted in Thomas H. Jukes, "DDT, Human Health, and the Environment," *Environmental Affairs* 1 (November 1971): 534–64.

24. For an earlier discussion of this thesis, see Harold Sprout, "The Environmental Crisis in the Context of American Politics," pp. 87–100 of *Ecology and Politics in America's Environmental Crisis*, Policy Memorandum no. 37 (Princeton, N.J.: Center of International Studies, Princeton University, August 1970); reprinted in Roos, ed., *Politics of Ecosuicide*, pp. 41–50.

Chapter 9

1. *The World We Have Lost* is the title of a remarkable book by the British historian Peter Laslett, who has unearthed long-neglected evidence of nonelite styles of living in preindustrial England and compared the hazards of that vanished milieu with those in comparable industrial communities. (New York: Charles Scribner's Sons, 1965.)

2. For a classic example of this scenario, see Norman MacRae, "America's Third Century," *Economist* (London), October 25, 1976, pp. 3–44.

3. An early and leading advocate of this scenario is Harrison Brown, whose views were considered in further detail in chapter 4. His most recent version (as of 1977) is "Day of Reckoning," *R. F. Illustrated*, December 1976, a statement addressed to the staff of the Rockefeller Foundation. Numerous other well-known scientists share in varying degree Brown's image of the catastrophic consequences of a war fought with nuclear weapons.

4. See G. Evelyn Hutchinson's concise summary in the introductory chapter (especially p. 11) of *The Biosphere* (San Francisco: W. H. Freeman & Co., 1970). This book is a collection of eleven scientific articles originally published in *Scientific American*, September 1970.

5. Donella M. Meadows et al., *The Limits to Growth* (New York: Universe Books, 1972).

6. William Ophuls, "The Return of Leviathan," *Bulletin of the Atomic Scientists*, March 1973, pp. 50–52; Ophuls, "Reversal Is the Law of Tao: The Imminent Resurrection of Political Philosophy," in Stuart S. Nagel, Jr., ed., *Environmental Politics* (New York: Praeger Publishers, 1974).

7. For a popular but accurate description of the lifeboat ethic and triage strategy, see Wade Green, "Triage: Who Shall Be Fed? Who Shall Starve?" *New York Times Magazine*, January 5, 1975. For a critical response, see Harvard demographer Roger Revelle, "The Ghost at the Feast," *Science*, November 15, 1974, p. 589. For two low-key, carefully reasoned critiques, see Alan Berg, "The Trouble with Triage," *New York Times Magazine*, June 15, 1975; and Barbara Ward, "Not Triage, but Investment in People, Food, and Water," *New York Times*, November 15, 1976, op. ed.

8. The qualifying phrase, "in a material sense," leaves open the question, raised by Boulding and others, whether there may also be limits to the extension of knowledge and how such limits (if they do or do not exist) might affect human ability to manage social behavior as well as to tamper with nature in ways and to a degree unknown today.

9. W. H. Murdy, "Anthropocentrism: A Modern Version," *Science*, March 28, 1975, pp. 1168–72, especially p. 1171.

10. Assessing the American record with regard to energy alone, the editor of *Science*, Philip Abelson, noted: "great promises to the world that have proved repeatedly to be only idle words. . . . Instead of working for conservation, Congress encouraged consumption by rolling back the price of oil." He also cited other indicators of the failure to take the energy crisis seriously. *Science*, November 12, 1976, p. 681.

11. Marc H. Ross and Robert H. Williams, "Energy Efficiency: Our Most Underrated Energy Resource," *Bulletin of the Atomic Scientists*, November 1976, pp. 30–38. Many other assessments reach the same conclusion.

12. "Half-Way House," anonymous editorial commentary on Quarles, *Cleaning Up America* (Boston: Houghton Mifflin Co., 1976), the review appearing in the *Economist* (London), November 20, 1976.

Epilogue

1. Isaiah Bowman, *Geography in Relation to the Social Sciences* (New York: Charles Scribner's Sons, 1934), p. 4.

2. Aldo Leopold, *A Sand County Almanac* (New York: Oxford University Press, 1949); quotation from Sierra/Ballantine Books edition (New York, 1970), pp. 257, 263–64.

3. Philip Morrison, in review of Sir Bernard Lovell's biographical sketch of the British scientist P. M. S. Blackett, *Scientific American*, October 1976, pp. 138–39, quotation from p. 139.

4. Sir Charles P. Snow, *The Two Cultures and the Scientific Revolution* (Cambridge, Eng.: Cambridge University Press, 1959).

5. *Troilus and Cressida*, act 1, scene 3, lines 101, 103, 109–10.

6. E. F. Schumacher, *Small Is Beautiful* (New York: Harper & Row, 1973).

7. Scores of such assessments could be cited. One of the more impressive was the report to Congress (privately printed, 1975), entitled *Military Policy and Budget Priorities*, which carried the endorsements of more than twenty former high-ranking military officers and civil officials.

8. Joseph Wood Krutch, *The Grand Canyon and All Its Yesterdays* (New York: William Sloane Associates, 1956), p. 276.

Index

PUBLICATIONS SPONSORED BY
THE CENTER OF INTERNATIONAL STUDIES

Gabriel A. Almond, *The Appeals of Communism* (Princeton University Press, 1954)

William W. Kaufmann, ed., *Military Policy and National Security* (Princeton University Press, 1956)

Klaus Knorr, *The War Potential of Nations* (Princeton University Press, 1956)

Lucian W. Pye, *Guerrilla Communism in Malaya* (Princeton University Press, 1956)

Charles De Visscher, *Theory and Reality in Public International Law*, trans. by P. E. Corbett (Princeton University Press, 1957; rev. ed. 1968)

Bernard C. Cohen, *The Political Process and Foreign Policy: The Making of the Japanese Peace Settlement* (Princeton University Press, 1957)

Myron Weiner, *Party Politics in India: The Development of a Multi-Party System* (Princeton University Press, 1957)

Percy E. Corbett, *Law in Diplomacy* (Princeton University Press, 1959)

Rolf Sannwald and Jacques Stohler, *Economic Integration: Theoretical Assumptions and Consequences of European Unification*, trans. by Herman Karreman (Princeton University Press, 1959)

Klaus Knorr, ed., *NATO and American Security* (Princeton University Press, 1959)

Gabriel A. Almond and James S. Coleman, eds., *The Politics of the Developing Areas* (Princeton University Press, 1960)

Herman Kahn, *On Thermonuclear War* (Princeton University Press, 1960)

Sidney Verba, *Small Groups and Political Behavior: A Study of Leadership* (Princeton University Press, 1961)

Robert J. C. Butow, *Tojo and the Coming of the War* (Princeton University Press, 1961)

Glenn H. Snyder, *Deterrence and Defense: Toward a Theory of National Security* (Princeton University Press, 1961)

Klaus Knorr and Sidney Verba, eds., *The International System: Theoretical Essays* (Princeton University Press, 1961)

Peter Paret and John W. Shy, *Guerrillas in the 1960's* (Praeger, 1962)

George Modelski, *A Theory of Foreign Policy* (Praeger, 1962)

Klaus Knorr and Thornton Read, eds., *Limited Strategic War* (Praeger, 1963)

Frederick S. Dunn, *Peace-Making and the Settlement with Japan* (Princeton University Press, 1963)

Arthur L. Burns and Nina Heathcote, *Peace Keeping by United Nations Forces* (Praeger, 1963)

Richard A. Falk, *Law, Morality, and War in the Contemporary World* (Praeger, 1963)

James N. Rosenau, *National Leadership and Foreign Policy: A Case Study in the Mobilization of Public Support* (Princeton University Press, 1963)

Gabriel A. Almond and Sidney Verba, *The Civic Culture: Political Attitudes and Democracy in Five Nations* (Princeton University Press, 1963)

Bernard C. Cohen, *The Press and Foreign Policy* (Princeton University Press, 1963)

Richard L. Sklar, *Nigerian Political Parties: Power in an Emergent African Nation* (Princeton University Press, 1963)

Peter Paret, *French Revolutionary Warfare from Indochina to Algeria: The Analysis of a Political and Military Doctrine* (Praeger, 1964)

Harry Eckstein, ed., *Internal War: Problems and Approaches* (Free Press, 1964)

Cyril E. Black and Thomas P. Thornton, eds., *Communism and Revolution: The Strategic Uses of Political Violence* (Princeton University Press, 1964)

Miriam Camps, *Britain and the European Community, 1955–1963* (Princeton University Press, 1964)

Thomas P. Thornton, ed., *The Third World in Soviet Perspective: Studies by Soviet Writers on the Developing Areas* (Princeton University Press, 1964)

James N. Rosenau, ed., *International Aspects of Civil Strife* (Princeton University Press, 1964)

Sidney I. Ploss, *Conflict and Decision-Making in Soviet Russia: A Case Study of Agricultural Policy, 1953–1963* (Princeton University Press, 1965)

Richard A. Falk and Richard J. Barnet, eds., *Security in Disarmament* (Princeton University Press, 1965)

Karl von Vorys, *Political Development in Pakistan* (Princeton University Press, 1965)

Harold and Margaret Sprout, *The Ecological Perspective on Human Affairs, with Special Reference to International Politics* (Princeton University Press, 1965)

Klaus Knorr, *On the Uses of Military Power in the Nuclear Age* (Princeton University Press, 1966)

Harry Eckstein, *Division and Cohesion in Democracy: A Study of Norway* (Princeton University Press, 1966)

Cyril E. Black, *The Dynamics of Modernization: A Study in Comparative History* (Harper and Row, 1966)

Peter Kunstadter, ed., *Southeast Asian Tribes, Minorities, and Nations* (Princeton University Press, 1967)

E. Victor Wolfenstein, *The Revolutionary Personality: Lenin, Trotsky, Gandhi* (Princeton University Press, 1967)

Leon Gordenker, *The UN Secretary-General and the Maintenance of Peace* (Columbia University Press, 1967)

Oran R. Young, *The Intermediaries: Third Parties in International Crises* (Princeton University Press, 1967)

James N. Rosenau, ed., *Domestic Sources of Foreign Policy* (Free Press, 1967)

Richard F. Hamilton, *Affluence and the French Worker in the Fourth Republic* (Princeton University Press, 1967)

Linda B. Miller, *World Order and Local Disorder: The United Nations and Internal Conflicts* (Princeton University Press, 1967)

Henry Bienen, *Tanzania: Party Transformation and Economic Development* (Princeton University Press, 1967)

Wolfram F. Hanrieder, *West German Foreign Policy, 1949–1963: International Pressures and Domestic Response* (Stanford University Press, 1967)

Richard H. Ullman, *Britain and the Russian Civil War: November 1918–February 1920* (Princeton University Press, 1968)

Robert Gilpin, *France in the Age of the Scientific State* (Princeton University Press, 1968)

William B. Bader, *The United States and the Spread of Nuclear Weapons* (Pegasus, 1968)

Richard A. Falk, *Legal Order in a Violent World* (Princeton University Press, 1968)

Cyril E. Black, Richard A. Falk, Klaus Knorr and Oran R. Young, *Neutralization and World Politics* (Princeton University Press, 1968)

Oran R. Young, *The Politics of Force: Bargaining during International Crises* (Princeton University Press, 1969)

Klaus Knorr and James N. Rosenau, eds., *Contending Approaches to International Politics* (Princeton University Press, 1969)

James N. Rosenau, ed., *Linkage Politics: Essays on the Convergence of National and International Systems* (Free Press, 1969)

John T. McAlister, Jr., *Viet Nam: The Origins of Revolution* (Knopf, 1969)

Jean Edward Smith, *Germany beyond the Wall: People, Politics and Prosperity* (Little, Brown, 1969)

James Barros, *Betrayal from Within: Joseph Avenol, Secretary-General of the League of Nations, 1933–1940* (Yale University Press, 1969)

Charles Hermann, *Crises in Foreign Policy: A Simulation Analysis* (Bobbs-Merrill, 1969)

Robert C. Tucker, *The Marxian Revolutionary Idea: Essays on Marxist Thought and Its Impact on Radical Movements* (W. W. Norton, 1969)

Harvey Waterman, *Political Change in Contemporary France: The Politics of an Industrial Democracy* (Charles E. Merrill, 1969)

Cyril E. Black and Richard A. Falk, eds., *The Future of the International Legal Order*. Vol. 1: *Trends and Patterns* (Princeton University Press, 1969)

Ted Robert Gurr, *Why Men Rebel* (Princeton University Press, 1969)

C. Sylvester Whitaker, *The Politics of Tradition: Continuity and Change in Northern Nigeria 1946–1960* (Princeton University Press, 1970)

Richard A. Falk, *The Status of Law in International Society* (Princeton University Press, 1970)

Klaus Knorr, *Military Power and Potential* (D. C. Heath, 1970)

Cyril E. Black and Richard A. Falk, eds., *The Future of the International Legal Order*. Vol. 2: *Wealth and Resources* (Princeton University Press, 1970)

Leon Gordenker, ed., *The United Nations in International Politics* (Princeton University Press, 1971)

Cyril E. Black and Richard A. Falk, eds., *The Future of the International Legal Order*. Vol. 3: *Conflict Management* (Princeton University Press, 1971)

Francine R. Frankel, *India's Green Revolution: Political Costs of Economic Growth* (Princeton University Press, 1971)

Harold and Margaret Sprout, *Toward a Politics of the Planet Earth* (Van Nostrand Reinhold, 1971)

Cyril E. Black and Richard A. Falk, eds., *The Future of the International Legal Order*. Vol. 4: *The Structure of the International Environment* (Princeton University Press, 1972)

Gerald Garvey, *Energy, Ecology, Economy* (W. W. Norton, 1972)

Richard Ullman, *The Anglo-Soviet Accord* (Princeton University Press, 1973)

Klaus Knorr, *Power and Wealth: The Political Economy of International Power* (Basic Books, 1973)

Anton Bebler, *Military Role in Africa: Dahomey, Ghana, Sierra Leone, and Mali* (Praeger Publishers, 1973)

Robert C. Tucker, *Stalin as Revolutionary 1879–1929: A Study in History and Personality* (W. W. Norton, 1973)

Edward L. Morse, *Foreign Policy and Interdependence in Gaullist France* (Princeton University Press, 1973)

Henry Bienen, *Kenya: The Politics of Participation and Control* (Princeton University Press, 1974)

Gregory J. Massell, *The Surrogate Proletariat: Moslem Women and Revolutionary Strategies in Soviet Central Asia, 1919–1929* (Princeton University Press, 1974)

James N. Rosenau, *Citizenship between Elections: An Inquiry into the Mobilizable American* (Free Press, 1974)

Ervin Laszlo, *A Strategy for the Future: The Systems Approach to World Order* (Braziller, 1974)

John R. Vincent, *Nonintervention and International Order* (Princeton University Press, 1974)

Jan H. Kalicki, *The Pattern of Sino-American Crises: Political-Military Interactions in the 1950s* (Cambridge University Press, 1975)

Klaus Knorr, *The Power of Nations: The Political Economy of International Relations* (Basic Books, 1975)

James P. Sewell, *UNESCO and World Politics: Engaging in International Relations* (Princeton University Press, 1975)

Richard A. Falk, *A Global Approach to National Policy* (Harvard University Press, 1975)

Harry Eckstein and Ted Robert Gurr, *Patterns of Authority: A Structural Basis for Political Inquiry* (John Wiley & Sons, 1975)

Cyril E. Black, Marius B. Jansen, Herbert S. Levine, Marion J. Levy, Jr., Henry Rosovsky, Gilbert Rozman, Henry D. Smith II, and S. Frederick Starr, *The Modernization of Japan and Russia* (Free Press, 1975)

Leon Gordenker, *International Aid and National Decisions: Development Programs in Malawi, Tanzania, and Zambia* (Princeton University Press, 1976)

Carl Von Clausewitz, *On War*, ed. and trans. Michael Howard and Peter Paret (Princeton University Press, 1976)

Gerald Garvey and Lou Ann Garvey, eds. *International Resource Flows* (Lexington Books, D. C. Heath, 1977)

Walter F. Murphy and Joseph Tanenhaus, *Comparative Constitutional Law: Cases and Commentaries*, (St. Martin's Press, 1977)

Gerald Garvey, *Nuclear Power and Social Planning: The City of the Second Sun* (Lexington Books, D. C. Heath, 1977)

Richard E. Bissell, *Apartheid and International Organizations* (Westview Press, 1977)

David P. Forsythe, *Humanitarian Politics: The International Committee of the Red Cross* (Johns Hopkins University Press, 1977)

Paul E. Sigmund, *The Overthrow of Allende and the Politics of Chile, 1964–1976* (University of Pittsburgh Press, 1977)